CULT OF THE CAPTURED BRIDE:

How Ancient Women Took Power

MARY E. NAPLES

CULT OF THE CAPTURED BRIDE:

How Ancient Women Took Power

MARY E. NAPLES

Classical Wisdom Weekly

Cult of the Captured Bride
Copyright © 2023 by Mary Naples

ISBN: 979-8-218-10064-3
Ebook ISBN: 978-0-9861084-6-4

TO THE LOVING MEMORY OF MY MOTHER...
AND TO ALL THE UNTOLD
STORIES OF MY FOREMOTHERS.

TABLE OF CONTENTS

TIMELINE FOR THE ANCIENT GREEK WORLD

GREEK NEOLITHIC AGE

6800 BCE - 3200 BCE Known for the advent of agriculture for which women are believed to have played key roles. Based on archaeological and literary artifacts, most scholars believe that the feminine fertility festival of the Thesmophoria has its roots planted in Neolithic soil.

BRONZE AGE

3000 BCE -1500 BCE Minoan Era
Minoan Crete was the cultural mainspring of the Mediterranean until it was overpowered by the Mycenaean/Indo-European invasions from the north. Although the Minoans had a writing system (Linear A) up until now it has not been fully decrypted.

Demeter's origins date back to the Minoan Crete goddess cults according to most scholars and referred to in the *Homeric Hymn to Demeter*.

1600 BCE – 1100 BCE Mycenaean Era
(Late Bronze Age)

The Mycenaeans provoked the widespread suppression of goddess worship in Crete and on the Greek mainland. They are called the "first Greeks" because they were the first to use the Greek language. Often referred to as "the Age of Heroes," the advanced Mycenaean civilization had urban centers and a writing system (Linear B). Although penned in the Archaic age of ancient Greece, Homer's epics (*The Iliad* and *The Odyssey*) are believed to focus on this era.

As a possible male response to the Thesmophoria, the sacred initiation rites of the Eleusinian Mysteries sprang from the Mycenaean era.

EARLY IRON AGE

1100-800 BCE Greek Dark Ages The Dorian migration/invasion and the collapse of the Mycenaean citadels, no written evidence exists from this era.

ANCIENT GREECE

800 BCE - 480 BCE Archaic Age Archaeological and literary artifacts date the celebration of the Thesmophoria to the earliest Archaic age of ancient Greece.

Though likely sung as a hymn long before its written composition, *The Homeric Hymn to Demeter* was penned in the seventh century BCE.

Over time, changing mindsets about the prospect of death and the concept of a happy afterlife would begin to take hold during the latter part of the Archaic age and continue beyond.

480 BCE - 323 BCE Classical Age The Telesterian was built in the fifth century BCE for initiates of the Mysteries. The Telesterian was a departure from conventional Greek temples which were designed only to house deities and members of the priestly class.

323 BCE - 31 BCE Hellenistic Age The Thesmophoria was celebrated until the twilight of the Hellenistic Age in 31 BCE.

(B)CE = (Before) Common Era

LIST OF ILLUSTRATIONS

1. The marble figure of Demeter of Knidos, 150 centimeters (59 inches high) erected near the ancient port of Knidos in SW Asia Minor (present-day Turkey). British Museum. c. 350 BCE

2. The Peplos Kore was named after the type of garment she was wearing (peplos). 118 cm high (46 inches), marble from the island of Paros. Acropolis Museum of Athens. c. 530 BCE

3. Zeus of Athens (Artemision Bronze) recovered from the sea of Artemsion, in north Euboea. 209 cm high (82 inches). National Archaeological Museum of Athens. c. 470 BCE

4. Hades (Gortyna) from the Sanctuary of Egyptian Gods at Gortyna, Crete. Heraklion Archaeological Museum. c. 200 CE

5. Rape of Persephone (Apulian red-figure volute-krater) Hades with his horses and Persephone. Anitkensammlung, Berlin. c. 340 BCE

6. Demeter and Metaneira (Apulian red-figure hydra) An enthroned Demeter raises her hand in benediction to Metaneira who offers wheat. Anitkensammlung, Berlin. c. 340 BCE

7. The Ascension of Persephone from the Underworld (by Persephone Painter), Terracotta bell krater (used for mixing wine and water). Persephone ascends to earth, guided by Hermes and Hecate. Demeter stands at the far right. Her ascension induced the renewal of the planet. Metropolitan Museum of Art. c. 440 BCE

8. Demeter drives a horse-drawn chariot with Persephone. Relief of a reunited Demeter and Persephone. Selinunte, Sicily. c. 6th century BCE

9. Double Goddesses of Catal Huyuk, carved from alabaster and stone, Museum of Anatolia Civilizations, Ankara, Turkey. c. 6000 BCE

10. Photo of Sanctuary of Demeter and Kore in Corinth in Acrocorinth (highest Corinth). Temple was first erected in the 4th century BCE. 146 BCE city of ancient Corinth was destroyed. Temple reerected c. 44 BCE

17. The Daughters of Danaus by Fernand Sabatte, 57.1 cm x 153 cm (22.4 inches x 60.2 inches). National Gallery of Victoria. c. 1900 CE

18. Overall view of the Telesterion in Eleusis, Eleusis, Greece. The site of the great hall and sanctuary celebration of the Eleusinian Mysteries. 7th century BCE

19. Eleusinian Trio: Persephone, Triptolemus, and Demeter, 2.20 x 1.52 m (7.21 feet x 5 feet). Marble bas-relief from Eleusis. c. 440-430 BCE

20. Eleusinian Mysteries Hydria, The Twin Goddesses are reunited at last. Red-figure hydria. Museum of Fine Arts of Lyon. c. 4th century BCE

21. Red-figure lekythos showing a young woman throwing a piglet into megaron. National Archaeological Museum, Athens. c. 5th century BCE

22. A Greek Terracotta Female Votary Holding a Piglet, Sicily, 28.7 cm (11 inches). c. 5th century BCE

23. Apulian bell-krater illustrating scene from Aristophanes' Thesmophoriazusae Apulia, Attic Red Figure krater. Martin Von Wagner Museum, Wurzburg, Germany. c. 370 BCE

MAPS OF THE ANCIENT GREEK WORLD

Mycenaean Age in the Greek World 1600 BCE-
1100 BCE, Wikipedia Commons

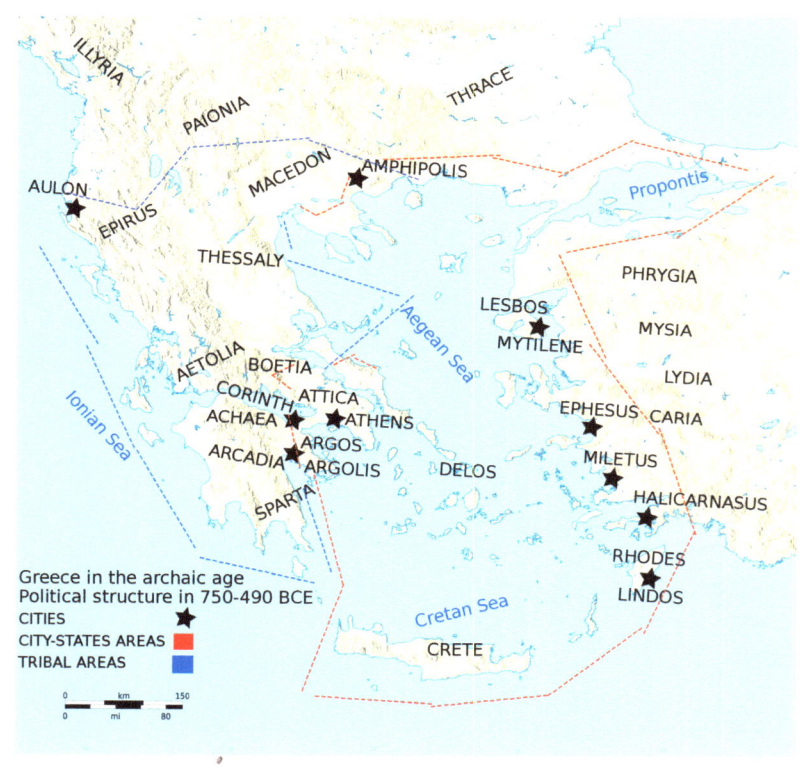

Greece During the Archaic Age: 800 BCE-
480 BCE, Wikipedia Commons

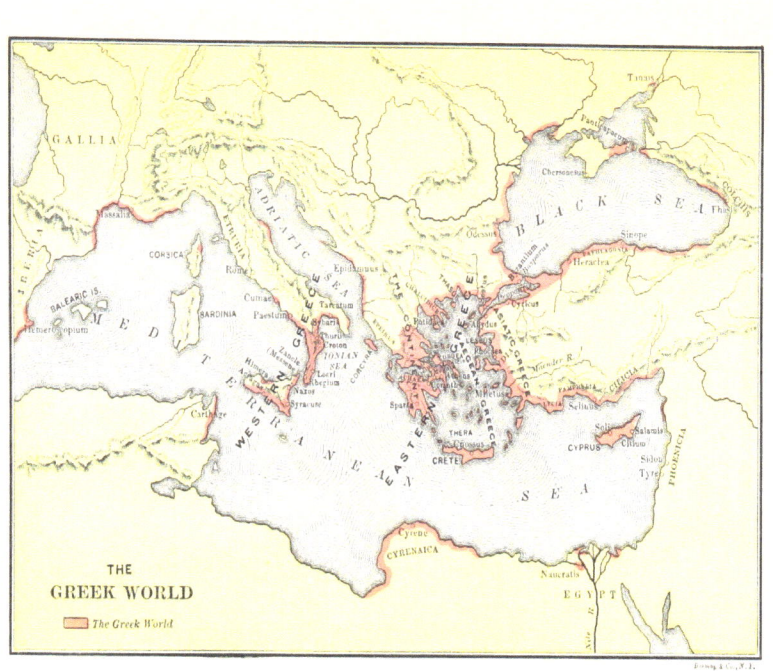

The Greek World, Wikipedia Commons

Athenian Empire at its height Classical Age:
ca 450 BCE, Wikipedia Commons

PREFACE

In a sense, this book was ten years in the making. In 2012, I began writing about the Thesmophoria for my thesis to earn a Master of Arts in Humanities from Dominican University of California. With an emphasis in women's studies, I had hoped to uncover the unsung contributions of ancient women and thought that fertility festivals could be a good place to start the search for a topic. The thinking was that as the festival's natural agents, women may have had some authority over how they were run. It did not take long before I discovered the all-empowering Thesmophoria—much more than just a fertility festival. The more I began learning about the Thesmpohoria, the more I wanted to learn about the Thesmophoria. With far-reaching implications, the citizen-wife adherents of the Thesmophoria had greater agency and more influence not only in relation to other feminine fertility festivals but also within the androcentric community at large. In this book, I explore the reasons behind the female authority inherent in the prehistoric Thesmophoria.

Fascinating as it is, examining a topic that dates back anywhere from two to nine thousand years has its distinct disadvantages. While much has been learned about the Thesmophoria, much more remains to be discovered. Notwithstanding the voluminous scholarship associated with the feminine cult, there are some uncertainties that come from the span of epochs, lost in the primordial haze of prehistory. Woefully, much in the ancient world is open to interpretation. Nonetheless, my hope is that the discussion of feminine empowerment cultivated by the Thesmophoria is brought out of the shadows and into sharper focus, with the expectation and promise of further scrutiny and more scholarship to come in the area.

INTRODUCTION

> "....marriage as the matriarchate recognized,
> is primarily an abduction, an acquisition—a rape."
> Erich Neumann, *Amore and Psyche* [1]

T he dawn's amber rays cast a golden glow on the hundreds of pious women as their procession passed through the cobbled streets. Clad in white robes and carrying torches, the sound of their fervent voices singing in praise of Demeter reverberated throughout the city walls. Faithfully, the people came out for them. From masons to magistrates, citizens and slaves alike packed the city streets standing elbow to elbow just to catch a glimpse of the spirited cortege as it made its way up to Demeter's sanctuary for the opening of their fertility festival—the Thesmophoria—one of the most highly anticipated religious festivals of the year. Throughout ancient Greece, from the Archaic to the Hellenistic eras (800 BCE-31 BCE), citizen-wives came

---

1   Erich Neumann. *Amore and Psyche: The Psychic Development of the Feminine* (New York: Princeton University Press, 1956, 62-63.

from far and wide to gather in their cities to celebrate their annual feminine fertility festival honoring Demeter, goddess of the harvest, and her daughter, Persephone, queen of the underworld. Primarily a fertility cult, the Thesmophoria ushered in the sowing season and was the largest of a series of fertility cults devoted to human, as well as crop, fertility.

In order to understand the Thesmophoria's influence, it is useful to examine what set it apart from other fertility festivals. The Thesmophoria was the most widespread[2] and the oldest of *all* religious festivals in the Greek world. Its celebrations spanned from Sicily's azure coast in the west to sun-drenched Asia Minor in the east, from the craggy mountains of Macedonia in the north to the deep recesses of North Africa in the south— possibly consisting of at least fifty cities throughout the Greek world.[3] The Thesmophoria's ubiquity in the region is testament to its prehistoric origins, predating not only the Iron age of ancient Greece (1100 BCE-31 BCE), the Bronze age of Minoan Crete and the Mycenaean era (3000 BCE-1100 BCE) but its rituals, props, and

---

2   There is even evidence of the Thesmophoria's observance in ancient Egypt during the Ptolemaic period (332 BCE-30 BCE) —-Sarah Pomeroy, *Women in Hellenistic Egypt* (New York: Schocken, 1984), 49.

3   Although there is evidence of fifty city-states celebrating the Thesmophoria, its observance is believed by many to have included up to one hundred city-states throughout the Greek world.

observances harken back to the advent of agriculture itself, with origins believed to be rooted in the Neolithic soil (6800 BCE-3200 BCE).[4]

At first glance it might seem counterintuitive that a women's fertility festival would be given such a high priority in androcentric ancient Greece. After all, women lived on the margins of society, removed from the public sphere. Despite this, or perhaps because of it, this festival would become vital. Indeed, the strict demarcation of gender roles may have actually served to empower women in ancient Greece. Fertility's all-importance in the ancient world meant women, as its natural agents, had the ability to capitalize on it.

So how did the disciples of the Thesmophoria form an identity around the cult, which promoted a feminine consciousness uncommon in the patriarchal dominion of ancient Greece? Against the backdrop of extreme misogyny, we'll review the esteem men had for the Thesmophoria and explore the possible reasons for it. Primary and secondary sources are used to substantiate the inferences made throughout. As background, Chapter One is devoted to the gynocentric narrative in the *Homeric Hymn to Demeter*—-a tale believed

---

4   Kevin Clinton, *Myth and Cult: The Iconography of the Eleusinian Mysteries* (Stockholm: Svenska Institute of Athens, 1990), 28-37; H.W. Park, *Aspects of Greek and Roman Life: Festivals of the Athenians* (London: Thames and Hudson Ltd, 1977), 82.

to have predated the written word itself. Primarily a woman's story, the myth is examined in detail exploring its anthropological aspects in the all-important area of marriage and how its overarching message of female empowerment resonated for women. Considered also are the roles played by the male and female deities and how they had corresponded to the lives of average Greek men and women, including a specific discussion regarding Demeter's origins and the antecedent action leading up to Persephone's rape. Through our deep dive into mythology, we will be able to catch a glimpse of our prehistoric past and consider the many parallels between myth and history. Finally, the last chapters explore the primeval connection between mothers and daughters, and how this primal bond relates to the myth.

Chapter Two analyzes the aetiological relationship between myth and ritual as it relates to the *Hymn* and the cult practice of the Thesmophoria is analyzed. Which came first, myth or ritual? It was the strong contention of Jane Ellen Harrison, a leading voice in classical studies from the late nineteenth/early twentieth century, that the Thesmophoria preceded the *Hymn* by some thousands of years.[5] Although contrary to our modern-day sensibilities of cause and effect, ritual preceding myth is a premise with which most present-day scholars

---

5   Jane Ellen Harrison, *Prolegomena to the Study of Greek Religion* (New York: Princeton University Press, 1991), 124.

agree. Whenever possible, primary sources are used to corroborate primordial rites observed at the all-secret feminine festival. For instance, the innovative use of plants enhanced the agency and feminine well-being of the citizen-wives; a practice that could even have relevance for women living in the twenty-first century.

The origins of the Thesmophoria are discussed in Chapter Three; including why most experts believe that the all-female cult sprang forth from the Neolithic age. It was an era famed for the advent of agriculture for which women are believed to have played key roles, as well as a time before the bonds of patriarchal marriage yoked women to their life's partner. Because Neolithic times preceded the advent of patriarchal marriage, it is believed that Neolithic women had agency in their lives. As a result, the festival's Neolithic origins were empowering for women in ancient Greece whose lives were tightly constricted. Believed to be a masculine response to the feminine Thesmophoria, the Eleusinian Mysteries will be reviewed in Chapter Four, where we will touch upon some key differences and close similarities between the two super-secretive rituals. Apropos of the Mysteries, Harrison argued that the Eleusinian Mysteries issued forth from the more antiquated Thesmophoria[6]

---

6   Harrison, 120.

—-a speculation supported by twenty-first-century Eleusinian scholar, Kevin Clinton as well.[7]

Finally, Chapter Five examines the sinister aspects of the Thesmophoria. Because the Thesmophoria was the only feminine ritual where sacrifices were made, the citizen-wife participants had access to instruments of death. This access to sacrificial knives and spits, along with the subversive elements of the festival, brought about stories of violence perpetrated by the citizen-wives against male interlopers. In a society where men set the rules, a community of empowered women armed to the teeth, struck fear in their hearts—which these stories affirm.

The Meaning of the Thesmophoria

While men viewed the Thesmophoria with wary respect, what did the Thesmophoria signify to women? Although typically confined to the seclusion of their domiciles, literary and archaeological sources suggest that, depending on their municipality, women in ancient Greece left their homes and families for anywhere from three to ten days (and nights) in order to participate in the Thesmophoria—an occurrence of particular

---

7   Kevin Clinton, "The Sanctuary of Demeter and Kore at Eleusis," in *Greek Sanctuaries: New Approaches,* ed. Nanno Marinatos and Robin Hagg, (London: Routledge: 1993), 110-124.

significance in and of itself. Most city-states like Athens, Sparta, and Abdera celebrated the Thesmophoria for three days, while in other cities, like Pella and Attica, it was celebrated for five. At ten days, Syracuse (Sicily) celebrated it for the longest. While most *poleis* (city-states) celebrated during the sowing season in the autumn, in some *poleis,* such as Delos and Thebes, the festival took place during the summer's threshing season.

Membership in the Thesmophoria was restricted to citizen-wives in good standing. Make no mistake, since women could not be citizens in ancient Greece, "citizen-wives" simply meant wives of male citizens who were also daughters of male citizens.[8] Moreover, "good standing" refers to wives who were not adulterous. Predictably, the double standard in ancient Greece was a matter of course. Unless he seduced another man's wife, a husband could commit adultery with impunity.[9] But such freedom was not granted to the gentler sex. In Athens, a wife was considered adulterous if she had an affair with any man— regardless of his marital status. Moreover, a wife who was convicted of adultery was ostracized; she could no longer share her husband's

---

8   Male citizens were a privileged class. In Athens, it is believed that only about twenty percent of the population were male citizens.

9   Sue Blundell, "Marriage and the Maiden," in *The Sacred and the Feminine in Ancient Greece* ed. Sue Blundell and Margaret Williamson, (London: Routledge, 1998), 48.

oikos (house) and was forbidden from participating in women's ritual events, such as the Thesmophoria.[10] No maidens, female metics nor female slaves were allowed in the Thesmophoria and although responsible for the expenses related to its celebration, men were strictly prohibited from attending any portion of the festival--at their peril.

In addition to their financial support for the Thesmophoria, men's reverence for the cult was reflected by the cessation of certain civic functions on the second and most sacred day of the festival. In Athens, the Boule Council—a body of five hundred who set the agenda for the democratic assembly—-was unable to meet. Moreover, law courts were completely suspended and all prisoners were released from jail. Indubitably, there were other feminine festivals devoted to fertility, but none as venerated as the Thesmophoria.[11]

---

10   Barbara Goff, *Citizen Bacchae* (Berkeley: University of
       California Press, 2004), 152."No woman was ever excluded
       from ritual participation so completely as the convicted
       adulteress."

11   There were three notable feminine agricultural festivals
       all of which honored Demeter: Skirophoria, celebrated
       during threshing season in the months of June/July (12th
       of Skirophorion). Stenia was primarily an Athenian festival
       celebrated a few days before the Thesmophoria. It was
       essentially a companion festival to the Thesmophoria
       where the sacrificing of piglets may have taken place.
       Haloa was a women-only agricultural festival, celebrated
       primarily in Eleusis. It was another threshing festival
       celebrated during the month of Poseidon (month six-
       June).

A Day in the Life of an Ancient Greek Woman— The Role of Women

To appreciate the significance of a feminine-only cult festival garnering esteem from the entire community—including its male citizens—it is important to get a glimpse into what life was like for women in ancient Greece.

A woman's place was in the home tending to things such as nursing children, weaving clothing, and preparing food. Because citizen-wives were hidden from the public sphere, even the trivial task of shopping was off-limits to them. With their every move directed by a male guardian, women were kept in seclusion and encouraged to be silent. Giving women the vote was never debated in this newly democratized society. Although called citizen-wives, the citizenship a wife shared with her husband was a watered-down variety merely entitling her to bear his children—most importantly his sons since male citizens could only be born from citizen-wives. In deliberating the rights of Greek women, Greek scholar and professor Barbara Goff asserts in her seminal book, *Citizen Bacchae*: *"Women (citizen-wives) had the ability to bear children who would-be citizens, thus to transmit what they do not themselves possess."* [12] Therefore, a latent or passive

---

12   Goff, 164.

sort of citizenship was the only kind doled out to the second sex.

Although women played a major role in the collective imagination of the *polis*, besides this form of passive citizenship, they were restricted from entering it. Even leisure activities were off-limits to them. While often represented in drama, female roles were played exclusively by males. Not only that, most scholars today believe that women were even banned from attending performances.

Men's Low Esteem of Women

Dating back to the seventh century BCE, the myth of Pandora according to Hesiod reveals how Pandora's curiosity led her to open a jar or *pithos* that would release evil onto humankind. But that was not the end of it, it was further believed that women were Pandora's descendants, and as such, were the consequence of an unrelated act of creation from their esteemed male counterparts. It's worth noting that not unlike Eve and the forbidden apple, Pandora was the first mortal woman whose action of opening a jar[13] thrust humanity into a tailspin by releasing evil into the world.

Of Pandora, Hesiod proclaims: "*She was sheer guile to be withstood by men.*" Adding, "*For from her is*

---

13   Although commonly thought of as a box, the myth states that it was a jar or *pithos* that Pandora opened.

the deadly race and tribe of women who live amongst mortal men to their great trouble, no helpmates in hateful poverty, but only in wealth."[14]

Truth be told, men viewed women as separate entities and compelled them, as slaves or foreigners, to remain outside the community. In fact, the opposition between male and female was a guiding principle in the Greek world. While males begrudgingly saw women as a necessary and vital element of life, women were also considered dangerous, disagreeable, and as an entity to be excluded at all costs.

This disregard is evident from the mouths of three respected Athenian males. In his famous funeral speech, renowned Athenian statesman Pericles (495 BCE - 429 BCE) argued: "*The greatest glory of a woman is to be least talked about by men whether they are praising or criticizing you.*"[15] And according to the sage Aristotle (384 BCE - 322 BCE): "*The male is by nature superior and the female inferior...the one rules and the other is ruled.*"[16] Lastly setting us straight on women's roles, an Athenian politician, Apollodorus of Archarnae (394 BCE - 343

---

14 Hesiod. *Theogony,* trans. Dorothea Wender (London: Penguin Books),1982, Line 585-588.

15 Thucydides. *History of the Peloponnesian War, Book Two* "Pericles' Funeral Oration" (The Hellenic Parliament, 1998).

16 Aristotle *Politics*, Book One Vol. 21, tr H. Rackham (Cambridge, MA: Harvard University Press; London:William Heinemann Ltd, 1944).

BCE), contended: "*Hetairai* (courtesans) *we maintain for pleasure, concubines for the daily care of our bodies, but wives to give us legitimate children and to be loyal guardians of our households.*"[17]The gifting of "legitimate children" by citizen-wives was one of the key reasons for male support of the all-female Thesmophoria. Nevertheless, in consideration of the poor opinion men had of women, how did women's alignment with the natural world serve their better interests?

The Importance of Agriculture

Salient to this discussion is the place agriculture had within the *polis*. In his book about the Peloponnesian War titled *A War Like No Other*, Victor Davis Hanson asserts: "*...agriculture was the linchpin of all social, economic and cultural life.*"[18] The seat of Western civilization, ancient Greece gave us its genius for philosophy, literature, and politics, and yet, contrary to this cosmopolitan image, it was chiefly an agrarian society where most of its residents worked the land. From the seventh through the fourth century BCE, farming was a commonplace occupation revered by the greater *polis*. In fact, farming was so integral to

17   Demosothenes, *Speeches: Against Neaera* (Austin, TX: University of Texas Press, 2003),chap. 59.

18   Victor Davis Hanson, *A War Like No Other: How the Athenians and the Spartans Fought the Peloponnesian War* (New York: Random House, 2005), 8.

ancient Greece that even the word *polis* (city-state) has two components to it: the "city" representing the city proper or its urban core, such as Athens, and the "state" corresponding to the agricultural hinterland, which for Athens was Attica.

In his Socratic dialogue titled *Oeconomicus*, the Greek historian and philosopher, Xenophon (431 BCE -355 BCE) pronounces: *"When farming goes well, all other arts go well, but when the earth is forced to lie barren, the others almost cease to exist."*[19] Indeed, the community's health was contingent on a successful harvest, but because the land tended to be non-arable, success or failure was often determined by factors over which the Greeks had no control, often making their lives tumultuous. But as important as a good crop was to the health and prosperity of the city-state, it was not their only fertility concern. Due to their expansion abilities they needed an ample supply of males to maintain their military commitments and they needed women, that is to say, citizen-wives, to produce the much-coveted male citizens in order to lead the city-state. Is it any wonder that the Greeks had such a preoccupation with controlling fecundity, celebrating several fertility festivals throughout the year? Representing the changing

---

19   Xenophon, *Oeconomicus* 5.17 quoted in Victor Davis Hanson, *The Other Greeks: The Family Farm and the Agrarian Roots of Western Civilization* (New York: SImon & Schuster Ince, 1995), 5.

seasons, most of these cult festivals were associated with Demeter, goddess of the harvest, who represented abundance in all-natural things. Their pious respect for a higher power associated with fertility allowed them a sense of control in their otherwise chaotic lives.

The Fertile Female

To a great extent, membership in most fertility festivals was limited to women who were its natural agents. Nevertheless, fertility's all-importance in the Greek world did nothing to dissuade males from deriding the feminine reproductive process which made fertility possible. Feminine health was the source of much ridicule in ancient Greek literature.[20] Activities associated with women's reproductive systems were considered unclean, vulgar, and always to be concealed from greater society. Moreover, even ritual practice to male divinities excluded women in various states of reproduction, because they were considered "offensive to the gods."[21] In contrast to this sentiment, the Thesmophoria celebrated that which the dominant culture considered polluted. In other words, the

20   Eva Stehle, " Thesmophoria and Eleusinian Mysteries: The Fascination of Women's Secret Ritual," in *Finding Persephone: Women's Rituals in the Ancient Mediterranean*, ed. Maryline Parca and Angeliki Tzanetou, (Bloomington, IN: Indiana University Press, 2007), 174.
21   Ibid, 174.

Thesmophoria embraced femininity and the mysteries associated with the powers of reproduction.

Despite the scorn the patriarchs piled on them, women exploited their gender roles by accentuating their connection with the natural world. Though excluded from the daily activities of life within the public square, cult activity allowed women agency. Meeting outside the androcentric social constructs of family, the disciples were at liberty to become autonomous individuals—as they had been in pre-patriarchal times. Not only did the Thesmophoria allow women to become independent agents, but it also empowered a united feminine community without male restrictions—a dangerous combination for the dominant male culture of ancient Greece.

In discussing how the rituals of the Thesmophoria were contradictory to the mainstream culture, Goff submits: "*Once women have an opportunity to articulate resistance in ritual terms, there will be nothing to prevent them from proceeding to direct action.*"[22] To be sure, enfranchised men were afraid of the anger of the subjugated female made whole by her participation in the Thesmophoria. But because the festival was considered sacrosanct while being (to some degree) the official business of the *polis*, men had to keep a pious silence toward it. Subverting the dominant

---

22   Barbara Goff, 136.

paradigm, the Thesmophoria was an autonomous enterprise which afforded citizen-wives a great deal of independence[23] to run a gynocentric community, hold elections, draft proposals, keep accounting and last, but not least, practice sacred feminine ritual—all without male oversight.

---

23   John J. Winkler, *The Constraints of Desire* (New York: Routledge, 1990), 194.

CHAPTER ONE

THE MYTH—THE HOMERIC HYMN TO DEMETER

Mythology, in modern parlance, may imply unbelievable or exaggerated stories, however the term is used here to refer to stories of deep and abiding cultural significance. While not all myths are associated with religion, most religions have some myth or story associated with them that make ritual meaningful for its adherents. Before delving into the *Homeric Hymn to Demeter* and its cultural relevance for ancient Greek women, a thumbnail sketch of the age-old myth of Demeter and Persephone might be useful for review.

Without the knowledge or consent of either mother or daughter an agreement is reached between Persephone's father, Zeus— lord of the gods—and his brother Hades— lord of the underworld, to allow Hades to kidnap, that is to say, to marry Persephone. After Persephone's abduction, Demeter is devastated at the loss of her daughter in the land of the dead. In order to negotiate Persephone's release, Demeter stops the seasons and the earth becomes a desolate wasteland. At this point Zeus commands Hades to return Persephone to Demeter's earthly domain. But before releasing her, Hades lures Persephone into eating a pomegranate seed. The mere act of eating in the underworld binds Persephone to Hades for a few months out of each year corresponding with the dormant winter season in this time immemorial tale about agricultural renewal.

Evoking early agrarian rituals which celebrated the primal mysteries of birth, death, and resurrection, the *Homeric Hymn to Demeter* has the distinction of being amongst humankind's first literary compositions honoring agricultural renewal and the great mother goddess tradition.[24] Thought to have been composed contemporaneously with Homer's epics,[25] the *Homeric Hymn to Demeter* was penned in the seventh century

---

24   Preliterate up until the eighth century BCE, Greek culture had been conveyed orally only—not by written records.

25   The sequence for the first literary compositions in the Greek world are believed to have been as follows: Hesiod's *Theogony* and *Work and Days* were penned in the early eighth century BCE, followed closely by Homer's epics. The Homeric Hymns are thought to have been composed about fifty years or so after Homer's epics were recorded.

BCE and is one of a series of thirty-three Homeric hymns which honor individual deities.

They are called Homeric, not because they were composed— or sung— by the poet known as Homer,[26] but because they employ the same meter used in the epics: dactylic hexameter or six feet per line.[27] These Homeric Hymns were originally sung as prayers[28] and while there is no record of a specific performance of the *Homeric Hymn to Demeter*—hereafter referred to as the *Hymn*— most scholars agree that a portion of the *Hymn* was likely sung at the cult festivals honoring Demeter.[29] There are twenty-two adaptations of Demeter's myth, but the *Hymn* is considered to be of the greatest antiquity and for this reason, thought to be closest to the cult practice of the Thesmophoria.[30] In a nod to its primordial origins, some aspects of the *Hymn* invoke the Thesmophoria; meaning that the Thesmophoria was practiced before the *Hymn* was composed. In a causality that may appear contrary to modern-day sensibilities, scholars now believe that portions of the myth were used as justification for some of the rituals

---

26   By some accounts, Homer was a wandering minstrel who sang the epics we know as the *Iliad* and the *Odyssey*.

27   Helene P. Foley, ed, *The Homeric Hymn to Demeter* (Princeton University Press: New Jersey, 1994), 29.

28   Ibid, 28.

29   Ibid, 28.

30   Ibid, 97; Clinton, 120.

in the Thesmophoria. That being the case, the ritual is thought to have preceded the mythology.[31]

One example of where mythology is a reflection of history in the *Hymn* is when Demeter (see Figure 1) tells of her forceful abduction from Crete: "*I am from Crete, over the sea's wide back—not willingly; but pirates brought me thence by force of strength.*"[32] With her pre-Hellenic attributes, Demeter is one of the oldest of the Olympian gods with origins dating back to the Minoan Crete (3000 BCE- 1500 BCE) goddess cults. As a hypothesized matricentric society, Crete was the cultural mainspring of the Mediterranean until it was overpowered by the Mycenaeans (1600 BCE-1100 BCE).[33] As is often the case when one culture subsumes another, the invader gods raped or married the indigenous goddesses replacing matricentric elements with patriarchal ones. By rewriting the mythology, the Mycenaeans provoked the systemic suppression of goddess worship.[34] This eventually gave rise to a cultural shift that would encompass the widespread denigration

---

31   Harrison, 124.

32   Foley, 8.

33   Mara Lynn Keller, "The Eleusinian Mysteries of Demeter and Persephone: Fertility, Sexuality, and Rebirth." *Journal of Feminist Studies in Religion* 4, no. 1 (1988): 44. http://www.jstor.org/stable/25002068.

34   A member of the Indo-European peoples, the Mycenaeans entered the Greek mainland from the north in the second millennium BCE.

of women aptly demonstrated by the overarching rape myths.[35]

The Story of Demeter and Persephone

One of the oldest of these myths is recounted in the *Iliad* and serves as antecedent action leading up to the events in the *Hymn*. In an effort to reassure the long-suffering Hera that he prefers her above all others, the almighty Zeus proceeds to tell her about his sexual exploits, naming his sister, Demeter, in his labyrinthine list of conquests. But there is more to the story than that. In the *Odyssey*, Calypso tells of how Demeter made love to the Cretan youth Iasion "*without disguise,*" preferring the mortal over the ever-powerful Zeus. "*Demeter with the cornrows in her hair indulged her own desire, and she made love with Iasion in triple-furrowed fields—till Zeus found out, hurled a flashing flame, and killed him.*" [36] Thus, the god of sky and thunder jealously struck Iasion dead with a thunderbolt. In another tradition, after striking Iason dead, he rapes his sister Demeter.

---

35   Keller, 44; Marcia W. D-S. Dobson, "Ritual Death, Patriarchal Violence, and Female Relationships in the Hymn to Demeter and Inanna" *NWSA Journal* 5, no. 1 (1992): 49. "There is no question that the Hymn offers evidence for a violent patriarchal takeover which has reverberations on relationships between women."

36   Homer,*The Odyssey* tr. Emily Wilson (New York: W.W. Norton & Company, Inc, 2018), p184, Book 5, 125-128.

Demeter and Zeus never married. Zeus would have been husband to hundreds if he had married everyone he raped. [37]

The product of that rape was Persephone (see Figure 2). Persephone, initially known by the generic name, Kore or maiden, is famously abducted, and it is this story we will focus on. Predictably for this hyper-patriarchal culture, it is only after the rape/marriage that she is given the name, Persephone, thus an identity. The *Hymn*'s opening stanza refers to Persephone's abduction and the dark bargain made by Zeus and Hades without the knowledge or approval of Demeter: "*…the fair-tressed awesome goddess, herself and her slim-ankled daughter whom Aidoneus (Hades) seized; Zeus, heavy-thundering and mighty voiced, gave her, without the consent of Demeter of the bright fruit and golden sword.*" [38] Make no mistake, his being an absentee father did not stop Zeus (see Figure 3) from arranging the marriage of his daughter to his brother, Persephone's uncle—Hades, lord of the underworld (see Figure 4).[39]

---

37 Marriage and rape were so equivalent in the Greek world that ancients tell of military campaigns undertaken for the express purpose of rape and wife acquisition. Like Rome's mythological Rape of the Sabines, women were part and parcel of the spoils of war and were used according to men's needs as noted time and again in Greek literature.

38 Foley 1-5.

39 "Host-to-many, the many-named son of Kronos" Hades was also known by the Greek names of Aïdōneús, Aides and Plouton. Both feared and disliked in the ancient world, he is seldom depicted in art from the era.

Unaware that her life was soon to change irrevocably, a fresh-faced and carefree Persephone (Kore) wearing the flowing robes of a young maiden was picking flowers in a lush and fragrant meadow with her girlfriends. In her basket were the first flowers of the season: pale roses, violet-hued crocuses, blue irises, and finally, the yellow and white daffodils known in antiquity as narcissus. But narcissus was different from the other flowers: *"From its root, a hundredfold bloom sprang up and smelled so sweet that the whole vast heaven above and the whole earth laughed...the girl marveled and stretched out both hands at once to take the lovely toy."* [40]

Upon plucking the narcissus, the pastel-blue sky turned dark with menace. Then all at once, the earth cleaved open and in a horse-drawn chariot, a bearded and grim-faced Hades savagely sprang out, seizing the young girl to be his wife in the underworld (see Figure 5):

> *The lord Host-to-Many (Hades) rose up on her with his immortal horses, the celebrated son of Kronos; he snatched the unwilling maid into his golden chariot and led her off lamenting. She screamed with a shrill voice...* [41]

---

40   Foley, 12-17.

41   Ibid, 17-20.

Common in primitive forms of justice, her cries summoned witnesses to the crime. In her commentary of the *Hymn*, noted Helenist scholar Helene Foley asserts that even in *Deuteronomy* 22.24-27 it is made clear that a woman who is raped is not held responsible if she cries out in protest. This convention is evident as well in Greek literature when, in Euripides' *Ion*, Creusa cries with rage against Apollo,[42] and again in *Trojan Women* when an incredulous Hecuba asks if any Spartan heard Helen's cries for help upon her "abduction."[43]

Persephone's screams by themselves, however, were not for witnesses alone. Because of the sheer violence of the act, she cried for her all-powerful father to intercede: "...*calling on her father, the son of Kronos highest and best.*"[44] As the progeny of the supreme god and ruler on Mount Olympus, who could blame her for thinking that Zeus would right the grievous wrong done and rescue her? But the almighty, all-seeing, all-knowing, ever-vengeful Zeus was deaf to his daughter's wretched screams: "*not one of the immortals or of humankind heard her voice...*"[45] His indifference, however, was only half of it. Being orchestrator for the depraved match, he

---

42   Euripides, *Ion* tr. Ronald Frederick Willetts (Chicago: University of Chicago Press, 1958), 892.

43   Euripides, *The Trojan Women*, tr. Richard Lattimore (Chicago: University of Chicago Press, 1958), 998-1000.

44   Foley, 20-21.

45   Foley, 22.

was as culpable as Hades for Persephone's torment, yet remained patently unmoved throughout her ordeal.

Though her father was unaffected by her cries, the planet was not and came to her aid by alerting her mother.

> *The mountain peaks and the depths of the sea echoed in response to her divine voice, and her goddess mother heard. Sharp grief seized her heart, and she tore the veil on her ambrosial hair with her own hands. She cast a dark cloak over her shoulder and sped like a bird over dry land and sea, searching. No one was willing to tell her the truth, not one of the gods or mortals. Then for nine days divine Deo (Demeter) roamed over the earth, holding torches ablaze in her hands...* [46]

In direct contrast to an indifferent Zeus, for nine long days and nights, an inconsolable Demeter with torch in hand wandered the earth in search of her beloved daughter.

Finally, on day ten, a primordial deity, Hecate—a pre-Olympian Titan goddess associated with earth and fertility rituals—informed Demeter of Persephone's rape. Although she heard Persephone's cries, Hecate was unable to see who brutalized her: *"For I heard a voice*

---

46   Ibid, 40-47.

but did not see with my eyes who he was."[47] Because his rays allow him to see the entirety of the universe in the daytime, the two goddesses seek the guidance of another pre-Olympian Titan god, the sun god, Helios.

That Demeter enlisted the help of two Titan deities in her search for Persephone is significant, as the Titans were the generation before the Olympians and had opposed the rule of Zeus. Helios augustly reveres "*mighty Demeter*" and declares it was "*cloud-gathering Zeus, who gave her (Persephone) to Hades his brother to be called his fertile wife.*"[48] Worth mentioning, in the *Hymn* and most versions of the myth, Persephone and Hades produce no offspring. Alas, the dark bargain made between Zeus and Hades is a misbegotten one. Furious at Zeus for making the perfidious match, Demeter withdrew from her home on Mount Olympus. Instead "*she went among the cities and fertile fields of men,*"[49] finally settling in Eleusis, an area to the west of Athens, well-known for its cultivable land.

Disguising herself as an old woman, she sat near the Maiden's Well where she met three daughters of King Keleos—son of Eleusis—who treated her kindly. They took Demeter home to meet their mother, Metaneira. Although imitating an aged woman, upon entering Demeter's celestial glow filled the room. When offered

---

47   Ibid, 66.

48   Ibid, 80.

49   Foley, 93.

a chair, the goddess refused to sit, until Iambe —a servant—brought her a stool to sit on. She refused food and drink, yet despite being despondent over the loss of her beloved daughter, Demeter found solace in the lighthearted banter of Iambe, "....knowing Iambe jested with her and mocking with many a joke moved the holy goddess to smile and laugh and keep a gracious heart."[50] Fasting and imitating Iambe's light-hearted banter are two ways the citizen-wives honor Demeter in the ritual.

Ultimately, Metaneira allowed Demeter to nurse Metaneira's newborn son, Demophoon. In order to steal a mortal from the lord of the underworld—the way he stole a daughter from her— it was Demeter's goal to make Demophoon immortal.[51] By making Demophoon immortal she hoped to do the same for all mortals, thus robbing Hades of his flourishing enterprise.

> Demeter anointed him with ambrosia like one born from a god and breathed sweetly on him, held close to her breast. At night she would bury him like a brand in the fire's night, unknown to his own parents. [52]

---

50   Ibid, 202-204.
51   Louise Pratt, "The Old Women of Ancient Greece and the Homeric Hymn to Demeter," Transactions of the American Philological Association 130 (2000): 43. http://www.jstor.org/stable/284305.
52   Ibid, 237-240.

Modern audiences might feel that placing an infant in a smoldering fire could endanger the newborn's life, but such was not the case in Greek mythology where fire is often used as a means of immortalizing humans.[53] For example, the hero Heracles was apotheosized by being incinerated alive on his own funeral pyre, while Thetis used fire when she unsuccessfully endeavored to make her son, Achilles, immortal.

Under Demeter's care Demophoon thrived and grew miraculously fast—like a god. But things changed when one night Metaneira witnessed Demeter place her son in a glowing fireplace. Upon seeing her son incinerated, Metaneira screamed--as any mortal mother would. Tossing off the vestiges of old age and rising to her full celestial prominence, Demeter threw Demophoon from the flames to the ground howling: *"Mortals are ignorant and foolish, unable to foresee destiny....I would have made your child immortal and ageless forever."* [54] Due to the deep indignity Demeter suffered at the hands of the mortals (see Figure 6), she ordered the Eleusinians to build her a grand temple on a rising hill with attendant rites to conciliate her enraged spirit.

53   Carolyn Tully. "Demeter's Wrath: How the Eleusinian Mysteries Attempted to Cheat Death," in *Memento Mori: Magickal and mythological perspectives on death, dying, the underworld, afterlife, ghosts, ancestors and mortality.* ed. Kim Huggens (London: Avalonia, 2012), 144–152.
54   Foley, 256-257.

All the same, Demeter found no comfort with her grand temple, nor did she find solace with faithful adherents celebrating and making sacrifices to appease her fractured heart. Notwithstanding the high honors befitting a goddess, Demeter still mourned the loss of her daughter.

Illustrating Demeter's resemblance to mortal women

Until one day, at long last, she realized her true strength lies in her fertility. So, she stopped the seasons and the fertile earth became a barren wasteland, *"the ground released no seed, for bright-crowned Demeter kept it buried."*[55] In fact, the image of the earth becoming a desolate and barren wasteland would have been all too familiar to the Greeks whose terrain, frequently craggy, dry and mountainous, was oftentimes inhospitable to cultivation. The menacing presence of a furious Demeter must have loomed large in the psyche of the Greeks who lived in fear of drought and famine. *"She would have destroyed the whole mortal race by cruel famine and stolen the glorious honor of gifts and sacrifices from those having a home on Olympus."*[56]

A previously indifferent Zeus was troubled that the planet he shepherded was withering away. Make no

55   Ibid, 306-307.
56   Ibid, 310-312.

mistake, the fate of humankind was of no concern to the ever self-indulgent Zeus. Instead, he was worried that starving humans would be less likely to offer adequate sacrifices and other gifts to himself and the other divine inhabitants on Mount Olympus.[57] So Zeus pleaded with Demeter to make the earth abundant once again. But she would not relent until the release of Persephone. Finally, Zeus interceded with Hades on Demeter's behalf and ordered Hades to return Persephone to her mother in the light of her earthly domain. Ever-obsequious, Hades adhered to Zeus's request but not before luring Persephone into eating a pomegranate seed. The mere act of eating in the underworld binds Persephone to Hades as his wife for a few months out of every year (see Figure 7).

A Myth For Their Time

Did the parable of the kidnapped bride ring true for women living in ancient Greece? Living under their husbands' patriarchal thumbs, women had become accustomed to being out of the loop regarding the marriages of their daughters. As such, it was not

---

57   Besides, Zeus and Demeter, the other Olympian gods residing on Mount Olympus are: Hera, Poseidon, Athena, Apollo, Aphrodite, Ares, Hephaestus, Hermes, and Hestia. Although an Olympian god, Hades was the only god not to reside on Mount Olympus, dwelling instead in the shadowy recesses of the underworld.

unusual for fathers to bargain with prospective sons-in-law about the fates of their daughters without the knowledge or consent of either mothers or daughters. The truth is that the commodification of women set up more meaningful relationships between fathers and their sons-in-law, rather than between husbands and wives.[58]

In her book titled *Women in Ancient Greece*, Classical Studies lecturer Sue Blundell posits: "*Marriage to a stranger, arranged by the father against the mother's wishes, and envisaged as a kind of rape, would have been a reality and not a fanciful tale for many Greek women.*"[59] When young girls were torn from their natal homes at twelve to fifteen years of age and forced to marry strangers twice or three times their senior a fine line existed between rape and marriage. In an institution exploitative to its core, the rationale for pubescent brides was that, like livestock, the earlier they began breeding, the more offspring they could produce within their reproductive lives. Once married, in a social system called viralocal or patrilocal residence, young girls were forced to reside in their new husbands' homes which could be a great distance from their natal homes. Hence, having contact with their birth family was often a rare occurrence. That being the case, for all

58 Sue Blundell, *Women in Ancient Greece* (Cambridge, MA: Harvard Univerity Press, 1995), 42.

59 Ibid, 42.

intents and purposes, the girls were symbolically dead to their families. Consequently, Demeter's sense of powerlessness against the abduction, and the suffering that ensued at the loss of her daughter, could resonate for most mothers.

A Woman's Story

Although males are present in the account, it is a woman's story. All the major roles are played by females, and the areas of concern; marriage, agriculture, and sacrifice are indubitably in the feminine domain. Of the *Hymn*, Carl Jung argues:

> *Demeter-Kore exists on the plane of mother-daughter experience, which is alien to the man and shuts him out. In fact, the psychology of the Demeter cult has all the features of a matriarchal order of society where the man is an indispensable but on the whole disturbing factor.*[60]

Demeter plays the role of the archetypal matriarch who defends her daughter against the unwelcome interference of males. Because of the reckless actions of the males, not only did the ill-fated match produce

---

60   C. G. Jung, Essays on the Science of Mythology, quoted in Carl Kerenyi, *Eleusis: Archetypal Image of Mother and Daughter* (Princeton, NJ: Princeton University Press, 1967), xxxii.

no offspring, but the rape very nearly brings an end to life on the planet. While their activities drive the events, Zeus and Hades are remote shadows, whose dark force propels the dissonance felt by the mother and daughter.

At its most fundamental level, the *Hymn* is a story about a mother's grief at the loss of her beloved daughter. Told from the perspective of the mother, it is more Demeter's tale than Persephone's. In mourning over the rape of her daughter, Demeter is also grieving her own rape and the loss of innocence at the hands of the transgressor— the same male responsible for her daughter's abduction and subsequent loss of innocence. The story is a generational one to which most ancient mothers could relate. At once powerless and inconsolable, Demeter appears more mortal than divine. Suffering profoundly due to the actions of males, Demeter is initially powerless to set things right. It is this sense of helplessness that drives her sorrow at the loss of Persephone, mirroring the anguish that must have been felt by mortal mothers who lost their daughters to marriage each day. An enduring tale, many believe that the *Hymn* comes closer to representing the issues faced by ancient women than any other literary work from the era.[61]

---

61   Froma I. Zeitlin, *Playing the Other* (Chicago: University of
        Chicago, 1996),142.

Demeter's anguish at the loss of her daughter is in marked contrast to that of Zeus, whose actions initiated the abduction in the first place. Bargaining with the lord of the underworld, who most would view as an agent of death; Zeus is indifferent to his daughter's banishment into the land of the dead. In other words, he is detached from his daughter's symbolic death. Though immortal, due to her marriage with Hades, Persephone is spirited away from the living cosmos and is compelled to live in the realm of the dead for eternity.

Is her marriage not a sort of death? In her article, "Dangling Virgins: Myth, Ritual and the Place of Women in Ancient Greece," Italian classicist Eva Cantarella submits:

> It is difficult not to notice the similarity between the myth of Persephone and the typical scheme of the rites of passage. Nor can one not be tempted to interpret the abduction as symbolic death.[62]

All things considered, carried off to the land of the dead by the lord of the underworld was as close as any goddess could come to death. Seen as a transition, the

---

62   Eva Cantarella, "Dangling Virgins: Myth, Ritual, and the Place of Women in Ancient Greece," *Poetics Today* 6, no. ½ (1985), 96. http://www.jstor.org/stable/1772123.

marriage of a maiden was also viewed by many to be a symbolic form of death.

In light of this, literary and archaeological sources indicate that the funereal rites for women and the rites of matrimony were eerily similar. Both used garlands, ritual absolutions, the shearing and dedicating of hair, songs, a feast, and the focus on the transition from house to grave or from natal home to husband's home. Why was there such a parallel between death and marriage rituals? Classical scholar and priestess, Marguerite Rigoglioso, in her book *Virgin Mother Goddesses of Antiquity*, argues that the death-marriage pattern is due to feminine opposition to marriage: "*Equating marriage with death represents an embedded grieving over the massive shift that has taken place to reduce women's autonomy.*" [63]

As an illustration, the contrast between Persephone's carefree playfulness in the meadow to her violent abduction into the underworld speaks manifestly about women's loss of independence. Evoking a period before the patriarchal institution of monogamous marriage, Demeter was one of the great mother goddesses in the pre-Greek world, which emphasized the bonds between mother and daughter. While more will be discussed on this topic

---

63   Marguerite Rigoglioso, *Virgin Mother Goddesses of Antiquity* (New York: Palgrave MacMillan, 2010), 12.

in Chapter Three on the Thesmophoria's prehistoric origins, most scholars agree that Demeter's reign as a divinity precedes that of her rapist, the patriarch, Zeus.[64] Although matriarchal rule is believed by many to be more mythological than historical, undoubtedly, early societies were matrilineal—meaning kinship was traced from the maternal line passing down from mother to daughter where lineage is, in fact, more demonstrable.[65] During this time, the notion of patriarchal marriage did not exist, hence the mother-daughter relationship was primal. Recalling a time before marriage, the matriarch viewed her child as a possession, while the father figure was largely a nonentity.

More on Marriage

Notwithstanding the parallels between marriage and death, how else is marriage characterized in the *Hymn*? Principally seen from the female perspective, marriage is portrayed as violent, painful, and worthy

---

64   However, Zeus's name itself is believed to have its origins in proto-Indo-European language possibly dating back to 4000-3000 BCE. That said, the cult of the twelve Olympian gods of which he was the head can only be traced back to the seventh century BCE whereas, the goddess known as Demeter is believed to have her origins in the mother goddess tradition of the Bronze era (3000-1100 BCE) Minoan Crete.

65   Margaret Ehrenberg, *Women in Prehistory* (University of Oklahoma Press, 1985), 64.

of defiance. The *Hymn* presents mother and daughter divinities struggling against an arbitrary patriarchal arrangement, which is viewed as both cruel and unjust. From Persephone's scream at her abduction at the beginning of the story, the females are distraught with the bargain made in which they played no part. When she discovers that Zeus is behind the attack, Demeter is justifiably incensed and leaves her home on Mount Olympus. It is only after the Eleusinians build her a temple that Demeter realizes her immense strength. In the final act, by applying her power of fertility— which she possessed all along—-she is able to retrieve Persephone from the realm of death. In discussing what the *Hymn* meant to women in the Greek world, Goff affirms:

> *The Hymn does not only display female power and anger and the cost to historical women of maintaining the system of patriarchal marriage, the Hymn pretends that the daughter will return to her mother for part of every year, and consequently provides an imaginary solution to real separation among women.* [66]

Daring to defy the will of the patriarch, Demeter does something never seen before in Greek mythology—-she resists the will of Zeus and lives to tell the tale. Not

---

66   Goff, 133.

only does Demeter survive, but she very nearly wins the battle. After all, for the majority of the year Persephone returns to the light of her mother's earthly domain. While the *Hymn* aptly portray patriarchal injustice against ancient women, it also provides a favorable outcome—- the daughter lives with her mother for a majority of each year. Though life can never return to the way it was before the abduction, by providing this resolution most mortal mothers would have envied Demeter's achievement.

In direct juxtaposition to the feminine perspective found in the *Hymn,* are the Homeric epics with an androcentric mindset entrenched in promoting patrilineal marriage. The *Odyssey* is emblematic of this as it chronicles Odysseus's ten-year long struggle to return home after the decade long Trojan war. Marriages, such as that between Odysseus and Penelope, are praised as the greatest source of happiness: "*For nothing could be better than when two live in one house, their minds in harmony, husband and wife. Their enemies are jealous, their friends delighted, and they have great honor.*" [67]

If they were bored or unhappy in their home life, men were free to pursue various avenues outside the domestic realm, but no such outlets existed for their wives who were tethered to home and hearth. The

---

67   Homer, *The Odyssey*, tr. Emily Wilson (New York: W.W. Norton & Company, Inc), 2018, 6.182-185.

Odyssey focuses on the fact that it took Odysseus ten long, arduous years to journey home to Ithaca, but the truth is he spent eight of those ten years living with two other females; the nymph Calypso and the sorceress, Circe. Meanwhile pining for her absentee husband, Penelope is representative of the faithful wife who patiently stitched away —-for a total of twenty long years. Although Odysseus's protracted absence left Penelope with the responsibility of raising their only son, she had no power in determining her fate. This lack of agency is demonstrated when the subject of her remarriage comes up. The epic is unclear if her remarriage is her father's decision to make or her son's, but one thing is certain, it is not Penelope's. If the complaisant and pliable Penelope represents an ideal wife, what do Demeter and Persephone represent?

Symbols of Fertility and Agriculture

On an etymological level, Demeter's character is intrinsic in her name. "*Da*" is the Doric form of earth and "*Meter*" is Greek for mother. As earth mother, Demeter is associated with fertility, but the Thesmophoria is believed to be more than a mere fertility festival. In "Thesmophoria and Haloa," an influential article which created heated discussion in academic circles, Nicholas J. Lowe argues that the Thesmophoria celebrated humans becoming civilized. Humans benefited "*not by enhancements to their own fertility but by becoming 'hermeros,' civilized."* [68] Because of her association with agriculture, in the psyche of the ancient Greeks, Demeter was responsible for civilization itself by allowing nomadic people to settle the land and, ultimately, to become a society. While Demeter is associated with agriculture, on a purely symbolic level related to cultivation, Persephone is a metaphor for the seed, which goes underground or lies dormant in the summer months only to be released again for planting in autumn. In ancient Greece, the grainseed was buried in bins in the earth, then opened and distributed during the sowing season for planting. That being the case, Persephone represents resurrection and the regeneration of life; from life to death and back again each year.

For that reason there is a mythical connection between Persephone's captivity and release with agricultural renewal; resurrection myths were often associated with rituals devised to encourage the renewal of vegetation.[69] Therefore, since Demeter represents agriculture and Persephone vegetative regeneration, the mother and the daughter dyad are closely linked symbolically.

---

68   N. J. Lowe, "Thesmophoria and Haloa: Myth, Physics and Mysteries," in *The Sacred and the Feminine in Ancient Greece,* ed. Sue Blundell and Margeret Williamson (London: Routledge, 1998), 154.

69   Frazer, James. *The Golden Bough (*London: Summit Classic Press, 2012), 426.

In artwork from the Archaic era, the two goddesses are often portrayed as double images of each other and known as the twin goddesses (see Figure 8), making it nearly impossible to tell mother from daughter.[70] Demeter herself makes reference to the resemblance when she says in the *Hymn, "The daughter I bore, a sweet offshoot noble in form."* [71] As younger and older aspects of the same woman, they represent the phases of a woman's life and are emblematic of feminine transitions;[72]women could identify with either being mother or daughter or both mother and daughter. In her influential book *Playing the Other,* Froma Zeitlin posits: "*Greece was alone among Mediterranean cultures in imagining an agricultural scenario of death and rebirth that features an exclusively female relationship.*"[73]

Likely confirming the close relationship between mother and daughter is the double goddess figurine of a mother and a maiden from the Neolithic era. Although they share the same torso, they have two heads and two pairs of breasts (see Figure 9). This mother-daughter

---

70   Harrison, 274. "Mythology might work its will, but primitive art never clearly distinguished between the mother and the maid, never lost the truth that they were onne goddess."

71   Foley, 4.

72   Foley, 101; Harrison, 272; Marija Gimbutas, *The Living Goddess*, ed. Miriam Robbins Dexter (Berkeley, California: University of California Press, 2001), 161.

73   Zeitlin, 1996, 10.

figurine was unearthed during the excavation at Catal Huyuk in southern Turkey. Thought to date from the eighth millennium BCE through the sixth millennium BCE, Catal Huyuk is one of the largest and best-preserved archaeological sites from the Neolithic era.[74]

The Matrilineal Succession

But the stages run even deeper than mother and daughter. A detail often overlooked in Greek literature, the *Hymn* honors matrilineal succession. The intergenerational relationships seen in the poem are between Demeter, Demeter's daughter, Persephone, and Demeter's mother, Rheia (Rhea). Rheia is the Titan mother goddess who is mother to six of those living on Mount Olympus and is, in turn, daughter to Gaia, Mother Earth herself, the paramount primogenitrix earth Goddess responsible for both Greek pantheons—the Titans and the Olympians. In the *Hymn,* Demeter is

74 First excavated in 1958 by James Mellaart, who led a team of excavators from 1961-1965. Mellaart was later banned from Turkey for antiquities smuggling in 1965. Prior to that, Mellaart and his team found that most of the figurines they unearthed were female and formed the hypothesis that Catal Huyuk was matriarchal. This later came under dispute. The site lay barren for nearly thirty years until it was reopened in 1993 by Ian Hodder of the University of Cambridge. Hodder and his team contend that Catal Huyuk incorporated neither matriarchal nor patriarchal rule, but had social balance between the sexes— indicative of a matrilineal culture.

twice referred to as Rheia's daughter, moreover, Rheia, as grandmother to Persephone, ultimately, plays a pivotal role in the story when she mediates between Zeus and Demeter in finding a resolution to the crisis.

Time and again in Greek literature, students of the classical world take for granted the interplay between the male generations of the various paternal houses. Overwhelmingly androcentric, this is particularly true in the Homeric epics where women play a minor role to their leading men. When maternal genealogy comes up at all in these epics it is devalued next to the paternal bloodlines. But in the *Hymn*, beginning with Gaia and ending with Persephone, the family tree is matrilineal and noteworthy in its omission of males.

Zeus as father is in the story, but his presence is worthy of defiance. In addition to putting Persephone in peril at the outset, Zeus was unwilling to lift a finger to come to her aid. Ultimately, Zeus's sovereignty was largely thwarted by the females, his superfluous intervention symbolizes patriarchal power which exists not only to separate women from each other but, more importantly, functions to suppress the conveyance of maternal genealogy.[75] In a society that separates daughters from mothers through virilocal marriage, not only was Persephone robbed of a loving mother, but she

---

75   L. Irigaray, "And one doesn't stir without the other," *Signs* 7.1:60-67, quoted in *Homeric Hymn to Demeter*, Foley, 123.

was robbed of a wizened grandmother and the thousand and one foundational stories about her foremothers that a matrilineal-rich culture would provide.

By setting off the basic conflict, patriarchy supplants the mother-daughter dyad in favor of matrimony. Maternal lineage was inhibited when the young girls were spirited away from their natal homes, often never seeing their mothers again. Foley maintains:

> *For ancient women, Demeter and Persephone may have represented the extraordinary endurance of the bond between women of different generations in the same family, a bond that carried women through the physical separation from their family that could so radically mark their lives.*[76]

Ultimately, matrilineal succession is restored in the *Hymn* when the bond between mother and daughter is seen as more powerful than that of husband and wife. Yoked to marriages over which they had no control, the *Hymn* was liberating for ancient women because the mother-daughter pair triumphed by subverting matrimony—-the dominant patriarchal paradigm.

---

76   Foley, 134.

CHAPTER TWO

MAGIC, MYSTERY, AND CEREMONY— THE RITUAL BEHIND THE NARRATIVE

The relationship between mythology and religion is, to say the least, complicated. When does mythology become religion? Or do religions create myths? Religion can be all -encompassing; in addition to containing mythology, it includes other facets such as rites, theology, and mysticism. On the other hand, not all myths are associated with religions. All of this has to be taken into consideration when trying to understand the religion and mythology of ancient Greece.

Robert Graves argues that we may often consider other people's religion to be mythology.[77] This convention may be most strongly evident in the area of ancient

---

77   Robert Graves, "Introduction" in *New Larousse Encyclopedia of Mythology,* tr. Richard Aldington and Delano Ames (London: Hamyln, 1968), v.

Greek religion. In spite of the fact that most consider the traditional foundations of Western civilization to be avidly traced back to ancient Greece, the religious practices and beliefs of the ancient classical world differ significantly from the monotheistic belief systems represented by the Judeo-Christian traditions. Perhaps because there is no written dogma in Greek mythology, nor commandments admonishing adherents on how to behave, ancient Greek religion may often appear to be composed of "doing" (rituals, sacrifices, festivals) as opposed to "believing" (adhering to commandments and other dogma)."[78] Consequently, it might often be supposed from a Judeo-Christian perspective that the Greeks were less pious or committed to their religion.

But in a culture that credits its very sustenance on the capricious whims of the gods, piety takes on a new meaning. This is because religion was an around-the-clock endeavor for ancient worshippers whose lives could turn chaotic on a dime; not only did they pray to their deities for support, but they were obliged to offer up sacrifices to honor and appease them as well. So vital was religion in their everyday lives that its practice was viewed as essential for the smooth operation of democratic rule. In her paper titled, "Feasts, Citizens, and Cultic Democracy in Classical Athens," discussing

---

78   Allaire B. Stallsmith, "Interpreting the Athenian Thesmophoria," *Classical Bulletin* 84.1 (2009), 43.

the *polis* of Athens in particular, classicist Nancy Evans makes a persuasive argument for what she calls "cultic democracy:"

> *Spheres of influence that we view as distinctly separate, namely political activities among humans and cultic activities aimed at the gods, overlapped in the lives and behaviors of the Athenians, and Athenian democracy could only function well when political and cultic activities were properly combined.*[79]

Given that religious expression was part and parcel of the daily lives of ancient Greeks, it is not difficult to imagine the indespensible role its practice must have played in the lives of prehistoric humans.

The Power of Primordial Rites

Like adherents of any faith, the Greeks practiced their religious devotion through ritual. While a student of ancient history might not fully relate to the ritual practices of the ancients, to the ancient worshiper, the transcendent rituals observed at festivals brought the

---

79   Nancy Evans, "Feasts, CItizens, and Cultic Democracy in Classical Athens," *Ancient Society* 34 (2004), 10.

myths to life by emanating the eternal.[80] By evoking the primordial era, the cult practice of the Thesmophoria accessed some of its appeal from its very genesis.[81] The citizen-wives of the Thesmophoria found empowerment in the mimesis of the prehistoric rites since prehistoric women were more autonomous than their Greek counterparts, leading renowned classicist Froma Zeitlin to espouse:

> *The building of temporary huts, the use of acts of woven osier for sleeping on the ground, the curing of meat in the sun instead of roasting it with fire and the inclusion of foods which predate those of the grain culture...all point to a primitive state of development consonant with the myth of time when women were in charge.*[82]

Implicit in the primordial rituals is women's authority in the Thesmophoria. For ancient Greek

---

80   Stallsmith, 43. What may seem as "mumbo-jumbo" to the observer could be the source of abject adoration for the devotee. Noted Greek scholar, Allaire B. Stallsmith posits that magic carries negative *connotations,* remarking: "*Put plainly, it is only other peoples' ritual activities which are magical—never our own,*".

81   While it is beyond the scope of this book, a worthwhile question to ponder: could the Thesmophoria's ritual practices give us a glimpse into some of the earliest expressions of organized religious devotion?

82   Zeitlin, "Cultic Models of the Female: Rites of Dionysus and Demeter," *Arethusa,* 15 no.1 (1982): 142.

women, the Thesmophoria bestowed a link to an era before patriarchy became the law of the land and women's role was supreme. As with all religions, transcendence with the eternal tends to get passed down from one generation to the next. This is believed to be especially true for the adherents of the Thesmophoria who rigorously kept their faith through the ages.

What Came First?

According to Harrison, *"(the rites of the Thesmophoria) were even more primitive owing to the conservative character of women...they were preserved in pristine purity down to the late days."*[83] Indeed, one element of the ever secretive Thesmophoria's appeal is that its very genesis harkens back to the primordial fog of prehistory. After all, Demeter herself was believed to have formed the woman's-only religion. However, the *Hymn* was actually composed in the relatively recent Archaic era (800-480 BCE), therefore is it possible that the cult practice of the Thesmophoria preceded it? Which came first, myth or ritual?

The aetiological order of myth and ritual is a debate that has been raging since Harrison, argued in favor of the ritual preceding the myth: *"The myth of the rape of Persephone of course really arose from the*

---

83   Harrison, 120.

ritual, not the ritual from the myth."[84] Contending that the Thesmophoria was of "*immemorial antiquity,*" Harrison's claim was that all mythology represents a means for explaining irrational rites passed down through the ages. In other words, myths were created after the rituals were in practice, giving adherents an understanding and acceptance of practices that may have dated back to primeval times. In light of this, it is useful to note that the rites of the Thesmophoria closely follow the events of the *Hymn,* indicating that the *Hymn* was written with the rites in mind.[85]

Harrison was not alone in espousing that ritual practice preceded myth. More recently eminent Eleusinian mysteries scholar, Kevin Clinton, refers to the *Hymn* as an *aition* (a story used to explain the origins of a ritual) of the Thesmophoria, contending the rites were in practice before the myth was composed.[86] Because the practice of the Thesmophoria dates back to the Neolithic era—-as most scholars now agree—female disciples throughout the Greek world practiced their

---

84   Ibid, 124.

85   Fritz Graf, *Greek Mythology* (London: Johns Hopkins University Press, 1993), 116. "Only occasionally do we have the impression that the purpose of an *aition* is to account for the details of the ritual" he goes on to add that while the similarities (between myth and ritual) are close the ritual act could not be constructed from the myth alone.

86   Clinton, 32.

religion long before the narrative known as the *Hymn* was composed. Regardless of the lack of a cohesive narrative for the early disciples, archaeological evidence suggests that the women of the Thesmophoria were considered religious both in the spirit of the festival and its sacred rituals. Practiced by orthodox women who "*kept the Thesmophoria as they always used to do*,"[87] over hundreds, perhaps thousands of years, the rites of the festival were renowned for their constancy.

The Thesmophorion and its location

The citizen-wives practiced their primeval rites inside the Sanctuary of Demeter, or the Thesmophorion, within their respective city-states. It is worth noting that not all Demeter sanctuaries were used exclusively for the Thesmophoria—yet her festivals (with the exception of the Eleusinian Mysteries) were for female participants only.

To provide an overview as to the scale of the sanctum, Corinth's Demeter's Sanctuary (see Figure 10) was situated on three tiers.[88] The lowest tier was a refectory or dining area with thirty dining rooms,

---

87   Aristophanes, *Ecclesiazusae,* http://classics.mit.edu/
      Aristophanes/eccles.pl.txt.

88   Nancy Bookidis, and Ronald S. Stroud, "The Sanctuary
      of Demeter and Kore: Topography and Architecture."
      Corinth 18, no. 3 (1997): iii–510. https://doi.
      org/10.2307/4390705.

complete with couches to accommodate two hundred people. The middle tier was for sacrifices and offerings to the double goddesses. A cavity within this area had the charred remains of pig bones. Because of their fecundity, pigs were often associated with Demeter and are believed to have been amongst the first animals domesticated in the Greek world. On the upper and third tier of the Thesmophorion, there were two stage areas with room for ninety spectators each. There was also a rock-cut well in this upper tier.

In Athens, the ruins are not as evident as in other *poleis*, as such, there is some dispute about where the Thesmophoria was practiced. Up until recently, it was believed to have taken place in an uninhabited part of the commons on the hillside of Pnyx— where the Athenian general assembly met. Classical archaeologist Homer Thompson excavated the area, arguing that the Thesmophorion must have been situated on Pnyx's north slope (see Figure 11). Not only is the north slope smooth and gently rounded, but it would also have been a dramatic setting for the sacrosanct festival while meeting all the requirements put forth in order to accommodate hundreds (if not thousands) of women and their huts.[89]

---

89   Homer A. Thompson, "Pnyx and Thesmophorion," *Hesperia: The American School of Classical Studies at Athens*, 5, no 2, (1936), 185. http:www.jstor.org/stable/146542.

Even so, the only real evidence we have for the Thesmophoria being celebrated at the Pnyx is a reference made to it from Aristophanes' play *Thesmophoriazusae* or "Women at the Thesmophoria." Although much about the Thesmophoria can be gleaned from that play, regrettably, a reference from a comedy is hardly historical fact. Recently, however, in a paper about women's festivals, Miriam Valdes Guia and Anne Stevens put forth that Athens' Thesmophorion was at the sanctuary of the Eleusinion, located on the Areopagus hill northwest of the Acropolis (see Figure 12).[90] Not only is there a temple celebrating Demeter and Persephone at the sanctuary but also an inscription in the vicinity which honors a priestess of the Demeter Thesmophoros for *"accomplishing her tasks well."*[91] The Areopagus was the location of the court where the highest government council in Athens met, thus it would have also met the requirements for the singular significance of this sacred event.

The Sacred Rites

Of course there were regional differences in how the festivals were celebrated, however, since

---

90   Miriam Valdes Guia and Anne Stevens, "Women Citizens' Festivals, Debates and Justice on the Areopagus (Athens, fifth century BCE)," *Clio. Women, Gender, History*, 45 (2017) 266-294.

91   Ibid, 273.

more is known about the Thesmophoria in Athens, we will focus on that *polis*. Although the location of the Thesmophorion is in some dispute, there is less debate about the rituals practiced there.

The first day of the Thesmophoria was called *anodos,* "way up" or "ascent" and refers to the torch-lit procession which leads up to the Thesmophorion, beginning the festival. While Demeter's sanctuaries were often on hills, there is a double meaning to the term "ascent". It also refers to Persephone ascending from the depths of Hades—the prime reason for the festival. By ascending the hill to Demeter's sanctuary, the women were imitating Persephone's climb from the underworld.[92]

Depending on the size of the *polis*, the sanctuary might have had to accommodate thousands of women who set up huts or shelters within its open space. In Athens, for instance, they were camped out for three days and nights. The primitive huts were a token of the great antiquity of the rites; returning to the primeval housing where ancient agricultural people once lived.[93]

The momentous second day was the fast or *nesteia* and recalled Demeter's grief at the loss of her daughter. *Nesteia* was a day of deep mourning when adherents

---

92   Matthew Dillon, *Girls and Women in Classical Greek Religion* (London: Routledge, 2002), 113.

93   H. S. Versnel, "The Festival of Bona Dea and the Thesmophoria," *Greece & Rome*, 39 (April, 1992), 137.

sat on their mats refusing food and wine as an act of mimesis for Demeter's fast in the *Hymn*. Seldom given license in much else within the public sphere, female mourning in groups was a common practice in ancient Greece where women were encouraged to lead in public grief as "*performers of the lament*."[94] Moreover, it was not uncommon for the mothers at the festival to have collectively either lost a child to death or a daughter to marriage, ergo they could identify with Demeter's grief at the loss of her beloved daughter.

It is on account of her grief and subsequent rage, that Demeter stopped the seasons, thus the connection between the planet and the goddess was turned on its head and her role as lawgiver was suspended. The opposition between the goddess and the planet led to an inversion of the norms both within the gynocratic society of the Thesmophoria and within the *polis* at large. This was felt within the *polis* by the cessation of certain civic functions. As mentioned previously, in Athens, courts of law and the advisory citizen body known as the Boule Council were both adjourned on the second day. Additionally, all prisoners were released from jail. This last item was seen as a magical means of

---

94   Eva Stehle, "Thesmophoria and Eleusinian Mysteries: The Fascination of Women's Secret Ritual," in *Finding Persephone: Women's Ritual in the Ancient Mediterranean,* ed. Maryline Parc and Angeliki Tzanertou (Bloomington, Indiana: Indiana University Press, 2007), 165-185, 170.

promoting fertility as it was believed that knots, chains, and confinement, in general, hindered fertility.

On this earth-shattering second day of the Thesmophoria, most scholars believe that the women participated in "shameful talk" or *aischrologia.* Bawdy talk correlates with Iambe's jesting, which lightened up Demeter's dark spirits in the *Hymn.* In fact, profanity was celebrated in the Thesmophoria and other Demetrian festivals associated with the powers of reproduction such as menses, lactating and childbearing; processes which were frowned upon in the male-dominant culture.

Classics Professor Emerita, Eva Stehle submits: "*In the Thesmophoria...these are sources of power; pollution correlates with women's sexual autonomy for* aischrologia *or foul speech and bailing both excite Demeter's reproductive vitality.*"[95] Countering appropriate feminine behavior, the shameful talk was a subversive act that was empowering for the citizen-wives who were expected to be shy and modest within their male-dominant culture. Further, shameful talk had a sexual component to it which may also have included the handling of artificial likenesses of genitalia, an ancient source suggests.[96] Once again, demonstrating

---

95   Stehle, 174.
96   Scholiast Lucian *Dial. mere*t. 7.4; Cleomedes 2.1; found in: Laura McClure, *Spoken Like a Woman: Speech and Gender in Athenian Drama* (Princeton: Princeton University Press, 1999), 215.

control of their bodies, the bawdy talk was believed to encourage fertility and was often associated with Demetrian festivals, especially those where women were gathered in secret rites or mysteries.

It was at sunset on the second day that the women broke their fast with a barley drink called *kykeon* correlating in the myth when Demeter broke her fast. Some scholars believe that the *kykeon* may have been laced with the ergot mushroom which has psychoactive elements common in religious practices for inducing trance-like states.[97] What is known is that in the Eleusinian Mysteries, adherents drank *kykeon* laced with ergot during their initiation ceremony to mimic descending into the underworld. In a frieze from a temple wall of Eleusis dating back to the fifth century BCE, Demeter and Persephone are each holding mushrooms, possibly indicating the importance of the fungus in their cult (see Figure 13). Since drinking *kykeon* was a significant ritual in the Thesmophoria as well, many scholars believe that the beverage must also have had entheogenic[98] properties for the citizen-wives, though there is some disagreement about the type of psychoactive substances which were used.

---

97   Hugh Bowden, *Mystery Cults of the Ancient World* (London: Thames & Hudson Ltd, 2010), 43.

98   Any psychoactive substance used in order to promote an inner experience with a divinity.

According to the *Hymn, kykeon* is composed of barley groats, water, and pennyroyal. The ancient Greeks roasted their barley-producing malt, which needed little or no fermentation to become alcoholic. The alcoholic beverage coupled with an already fasting state could impact the "doors of perception." Similarly, pennyroyal oil is known to possess hallucinogenic properties on its own. In large doses, pennyroyal can induce delirium, loss of consciousness, and spasms. In addition to its psychoactive properties, pennyroyal was both an emmenagogue (encourages menses) and an abortifacient (induces abortion), establishing it as a plant with significant relevance for the feminine fertility festival.

Plants For Power

In her groundbreaking article "Cults of Demeter and Kore," Oxford classicist Lucia Nixon proposes that adherents of the Thesmophoria had agency in determining the role plants played in their reproductive lives. "*Plants could provide an easily accessible way for women to regulate every stage of their reproductive lives (menstruation, conception, abortion, delivery, lactation, and menopause).*"[99] Archaeological findings and literary

99   Lucia Nixon,"The Cults of Demeter and Kore," in *Women in Antiquity: New Assessments*, ed. Richard Hawley and Barbara Levick (London: Routledge, 1995), 76-93.

evidence reveal that through their expert utilization of different vegetation, women of the Thesmophoria determined every facet of their feminine well-being. On account of the tight feminine community that formed around the cult, citizen-wives could safely share with each other sophisticated knowledge on the use of plants to either encourage or discourage various stages of reproduction.

It is ironic that male citizens willingly supported and paid for their wives to participate in the Thesmophoria, in order to ensure a lasting legacy since the procreation of legitimate male citizens was essential to the viability of patrilineal descent and the overall strength of the male-dominant *polis*. Yet for all their blustering patriarchy, is it possible that the vital area of population growth was left to the caprices of the weaker sex? Using their expertise in plants, it may have been the women who decided just how fertile they wanted to be.

There was, after all, plenty of motivation for women not to be fertile. Due to the tender ages of young mothers coupled with women's nutritional deficiencies and overall lack of hygiene, death from childbirth was not uncommon in ancient Greece. That being the case, it should come as no surprise that upon occasion many women may have acted to dissuade its occurrence. So, while women in ancient Greece could not determine who their marriage partners would be, choosing amongst a variety of reproductive options—unbeknownst to their husbands—was one way in which they took charge of their lives.

Knowledge of medicinal plants is an instance where women's restricted roles in ancient Greek society empowered them, since most men had very little expertise in the use of plants. In fact, this ignorance is aptly portrayed in the *Hymn* when Hades entices Persephone into eating a pomegranate seed so she is bound to him for a few months each year. But Persephone has the last laugh. Unknown to Hades, the pomegranate seed has contraceptive qualities. Indeed, no child would spring from that unholy union.

Just as Persephone reduced her fertility, at a renowned fertility festival, some citizen- wives might have desired to reduce theirs as well. Wresting control of their destinies from the very powers that sought to restrict them—-could oppressed women have had complete jurisdiction in the vital area of reproduction? The implications of Nixon's insights are profound and force us to ask—did ancient women have more agency in this critical aspect of their lives than some modern women do today?

Chaste Wives

In another apparent contradiction of the festival, citizen-wives slept on mats made of *vitex agnus castus,* defined as "chaste tree."[100] Perhaps ironically this herb is associated with chastity and is a plant that has anaphrodisiac properties (reduces sexual desire), yet is known to promote fertility by inducing menses or lactation.[101] The use of this plant in a major portion of their ritual indicates their knowledge of its utility in the festival; it suppresses their sexual urge while controlling their fertility.

Ironically, chastity comes up over and over again with this fertility festival. The women, known by the oxymoronic term "chaste wives" are removed from their husbands for a period of anywhere from three to ten days during the course of the festival. It is believed that chastity figures into the ritual as a means of curtailing women's sexual energies in order to utilize them for reproduction. Correspondingly, in an effort to make themselves undesirable, the women chewed garlic during portions of the festival. Salient to this, in a tradition known as "blood rites," some scholars[102] assert that by using appropriate plants the women coordinated

---

100   Defined is an anaphrodisiac hence the name "chaste." At first glance, it may appear ironic for a fertility festival but perhaps not so much for the empowering Thesmophoria where women are believed to have had agency in their reproductive lives.

101   Zeitlin, 1982, 142.

102   Carl Kerenyi, *Zeus and Hera: Archetypal Image of Father, Husband, and Wife* (Princeton: Princeton University Press, 1975), 157.

their menses so that they would all be menstruating at the time of the festival. To that end, the women bled on mats they sat upon as a magical means of advancing the earth's fertility during the Thesmophoria.[103]

While the women had license during the festival, there were two prohibitions as well. In an allusion to Hades of the underworld, although pomegranate seeds were eaten at the festival, the women were not allowed to eat those that had fallen to the ground believing them to belong to the dead.[104] This is due to Persephone being bound to Hades each year because of eating a pomegranate seed.

In another allusion to the *Hymn*, women were also restricted from wearing flower garlands in their hair, because Persephone wore such a garland when she was abducted by Hades. However, Persephone— like all brides on their wedding day—was believed to have worn a saffron gown (*krokotos*). In mimesis to Persephone, Guia and Stevens propose that young wives of the Thesmophoria dressed correspondingly by wearing saffron-colored gowns.[105]

---

103   Betty De Shong Meador, *Uncursing the Dark* (Wilmette, Illinois: Chiron Publications, 1994), 95; Riggolioso, 154.
104   Walter Burkert, *Greek Mythology* (Cambridge, Massachusetts: Harvard University Press, 1985), 244.
105   Guia-Stevens, 277. Aristophanes also makes reference to the saffron dress worn by young women at the Thesmophoria in his play about the festival, *Thesmophoriazusae,* line 941.

The Kalligeneia [106]

Though there was no wedding ceremony at the festival,[107] on the third day the citizen-wives celebrated the *kalligeneia* or "beautiful birth" symbolizing Persephone's resurrection or rebirth when the twin goddesses are reunited. It was a joyous day of celebration, exultation, and a feast, presumably with a sacrificed sow. The final stanza of the *Hymn* demonstrates the jubilation felt by the celebrants:

> *But come, you goddesses.....revered Deo (Demeter), mighty giver of seasons and glorious gift, you and your very fair daughter Persephone, for my song grant gladly a living that warms the heart. And I shall remember you and a new song as well.*[108]

Besides the reunion of the twin goddesses, it is only fitting that the *kalligeneia*'s celebration fostered joyous reunions between mother and daughter disciples as well. Moreover, on the third day the

---

106   While Kalligeneia is a nymph nursemaid of Demeter and Persephone, she is also a little-known nursemaid goddess used to invoke fair offspring—such as the resurrection of Persephone implies.

107   Far from celebratory, the abduction/wedding triggered the day of mourning the women enacted on the second day of the festival.

108   Foley, lines 490-495.

citizen-wives exchanged remedies with each other on their reproductive well-being; this was particularly so between mothers and daughters.[109] Classicist Matthew Dillon contends that on this third-day citizen-wives were calling on the goddess Kalligeneia for the fertility of their wombs which would have been the opposite of what transpired on the second day when the women were believed to have suppressed their fecundity by sitting on mats made from chaste tree.[110] Critical to the health and prosperity of the polis, as its culminating celebration, the *kalligeneia* served as a pledge to the city that breeding healthy citizen children and a bountiful harvest with which to feed them would be the festival's consequence.[111] The celebration of *kalligeneia* on the final day of the festival was so all-important and widespread throughout the Greek world that its absence was noted by Plutarch when he reported that in Eretria *"they did not invoke kalligeneia."*[112] Yet in the same sentence, Plutarch notes how the citizen-wives at Eretria *"imitated the ancient way of life."*[113]

---

109 Guia-Stevens, 286.

110 Dillon,113.

111 Marcel Detienne, "The Violence of Wellborn Ladies: Women in the Thesmophoria," In T*he Cuisine of Sacrificing Among the Greeks,* edited by Marcel Detienne and Jean-Pierre Vernant, tr. Paula Wissing. (Chicago: University of Chicago Press),138.

112 Dillon, 113.

113 Plutarch, *Moralia* 298 b-c quoted in Burkert, 244.

The Ancient Way of Life

"*Imitating the ancient way of life*" refers to the state before civilization when primordial people cooked their meat by the heat of the sun.[114] In this way the city-state of Eretria was not alone; throughout the Greek world citizen-wives of the Thesmophoria were famed for cooking their meat in this fashion. There are, however, other theories about what the phrase "*imitating the ancient way of life*" signifies which could prove enlightening.

Within the Orphic tradition, according to the Greek philosopher Sextus Empiricus (160 CE- 210 CE), Orpheus himself is believed to have declared that the "ancient way of life" was the state before Demeter, when humans engaged in cannibalism. The notion is that when Demeter imparted her gifts of grain she brought civilization to humankind with laws against murder and cannibalism.[115] Although only a few fragments from his plays are extant, Moschion, an Athenian playwright of the third century BCE, similarly posits that primitive men lived in caves and "*devoured each other like wild*

---

114   Burkett, 244.

115   R. Drew Griffith, "Cannibal Demeter and the Thesmophoria Pigs," *The Classical Journal*, 111, n.1 (December 2015), 137. https://www.jstor.org/stable/10.5184/classicalj.111.2.0129.

beasts" before Demeter, the grain goddess, showed people how to prepare food and lead a civilized life.[116] [117]

Cannibalism, however, was not the only practice that Demeter ended. In a similar story attributed to Theophrastus of Eresus (370 BCE - 267 BCE), before Demeter imparted her blessings of the harvest on them, the primordial people lamented that *"they were sick of eating acorns."* For the citizen-wives of the Thesmophoria imitating the ancient way of life meant cooking meat by the heat of the sun and eating pre-grain foods associated with the prehistoric time before Demeter— foods such as nuts, roots, and bark. In her whimsical book *Uncursing the Dark*, Betty De Shong Meador imagines the *kalligeneia:*

> *The women awake singing. They have survived the great trials of Thesmophoria. They have dared to enter the abode of the snake. They have sacrificed before her—her awesome power*

---

116   Sue Blundell *The Origins of Civilization in Greek and Roman Thought*. (Routledge 1989) 534-535.

117   The suspicion that early Greeks engaged in cannibalism has been studied by ancient and modern historians alike. For further information on this fascinating topic, I wrote a paper about human sacrifice in ancient Greece where the notion of cannibalism is explored: https://femminaclassica.com/the-highest-altar-human-sacrifice-in-ancient-greece/.

possessed them. She loosened the boundaries of ordinary life and shook the women.[118]

By participating in the rites which enact Demeter's trials and ultimate triumph, the ancient women are reminded of their power and the essential and vital role they play in both human and plant generation.

The Gynocracy

While their knowledge and use of plants was a source of emancipation for the citizen-wives, the organization and its ceremony gave women license as well. In direct juxtaposition to being restricted from voting in the *polis*, the Thesmophoria required citizen-wives to exercise their democratic rights within the festival. Each year the women of the Thesmophoria formed a council, chose assembly members, elected magistrates, and selected bailers— all from within their ranks. An *ad hoc* democracy or a gynocracy, this politico-religious cult formed a feminine *demos* where citizen-wives—as a condition of being disciples of Demeter—-were required to make their voices heard by voting.

In speaking of the tasks of the citizen-wives, Belgian classicist Marcel Detienne asserts: "*Every year in the demes, women choose from amongst themselves*

---

118   Meador, 99.

who will preside over the ceremonies and exercise the power in the Thesmophoria."[119] Epigraphic and literary artifacts dating from the third century BCE, indicate that the rites proceeded *"as the women have decided."*[120] The elected leaders of the Thesmophoria were responsible for governing the festival on the proscribed days and ensuring the customs were followed as *"established by tradition."*[121] Though excluded from the daily activities of the polis, cult activity allowed women agency within the Thesmophoria; they were in charge of running the cult by holding elections, drafting proposals, and balancing books, in addition to practicing sacred feminine ritual.

In most city-states, priestesses played a role in the festivities, however, the Thesmophoria was famed for allowing its participants to act the part of priestesses themselves. Salient to this, two of the most sacred positions crucial to the success of the festival were *antletriai* or bailers. Although not priestesses themselves, these two holy women took a vow of celibacy, not only during the festival—as the other disciples did—but for three days prior to its start. On the second, most sacred of the days— the *nesteia*—it was the job of the bailers to descend into the deep hollow of the cavern. Believed to represent the womb of

---

119   Detienne, 129-147.

120   Ibid, 138.

121   Ibid, 138.

Demeter, the cavern[122] was a common chamber within the Thesmophorion. But before the bailers descended into the core of the cavern, they made noises meant to scare away snakes believed to inhabit the space. Was there a real concern for snakes in the cavern or could snakes be a symbolic representation of males as some have argued?[123] It is thought that male banishment was the objective throughout the festival, since it was males who were responsible for the anguish felt by the mother-daughter dyad.[124]

Sacred Objects

After the bailers descended the cavern, it was their job to retrieve the "sacred objects" in an attempt to renew the fertility of the planet. The "sacred objects" included rotted piglets, fertility cakes—made from dough and shaped like male and female genitalia—and fir cones.

122　In fact, according to Adam Nicholson's illuminating book *Why Homer Matters*, he discusses how the words for tomb, womb, and cave all stem from the same proto-Indo-European root, which is significant considering the Thesmophoria's origins spring from the Neolithic period (7000-3200 BCE). - Adam Nicolson, *Why Homer Matters* (London: Picador, 2015),153.

123　Rigoglioso, 152.

124　Perhaps not uncoincidentally, to ward off snakes as well, the women sat on the *vitus agnus castus* or chaste tree mats. As discussed previously, since the chaste tree suppresses sexual desire, it is believed that the "snakes" the women expelled symbolized the male gender.

It is believed that the piglets were either sacrificed weeks before at another festival in preparation for the Thesmophoria called the Stenia, or that the piglets were sacrificed at the previous year's Thesmophoria.

In *The Golden Bough*, nineteenth-century Scottish anthropologist, James Frazer discusses the casting off of pigs into the caverns to be analogous to Persephone's abduction into the deep recesses of the underworld.[125] As previously mentioned, due to their fecundity and because pigs were one of the first animals to be domesticated in the Mediterranean, the pig was associated with Demeter (see Figure 14). Further, *choiros* or pig was a vernacular term for female genitalia. Finally, fir cones were used because pine cones were known to be prolific.

Encouraging Demeter to reproduce through the goddess's close association with death, the women mimic Demeter, the goddess of the harvest, by making contact with death—in the form of the dead or rotted piglets. In this venerable aspect of women's mysteries, the magic of the cyclical patterns of regeneration spurs the living from the dead and back again. The newly born humus[126] the bailers scoop up is symbolic of the power

---

125   J.G. Frazer, *The Golden Bough* (New York: Random House, 1981).

126   Humus is rich, dark organic matter in the soil created by the decomposition of plant and animal matter used in order to spur the earth's fertility.

women possess by demonstrating their ability, through Demeter, to generate life in an exclusively feminine cycle. During the rites, Demeter's reproductive energy is celebrated for bringing forth multitudinous crops without male input.

Sacred Compost

Ultimately, the "sacred objects" were then placed on the altars of the two goddesses and mixed with seed to be used as "sacred compost."[127] German archaeologist, Erika Simon submits that composting is "*a great invention of the prehistoric agrarian culture.*"[128] The magic of composting was discovered soon after the advent of agriculture. When Neolithic people observed that plants flourished when the soil was mixed with the decomposition of plant and animal matter, it did not take long before the practice of composting was put in place. In his seminal book *Greek Religion,* the late German classicist Walter Burkert, a leading voice in Greek studies, attests:

> *The manipulation of the decomposed remains of the piglets to achieve a good harvest is the*

---

127   Stallsmith, 7.

128   Erika Simon. *Festivals of Attica: An Archaeological Commentary,* (Madison, Wisconsin: University of Wisconsin Press, 1983), 21.

clearest example in Greek religion of agrarian magic...unquestionably there is a very ancient tradition here; findings from the Early Neolithic Age already point to a connection between corn (wheat) and pig.[129]

Agrarian magic, also known as the Mannhardt-Fraser hypothesis found in Frazer's *The Golden Bough* states that all religious ritual originates from concerns about fertility. While some might argue against fertility accounting for *all* religious festivals, there is no dispute that it was behind the Thesmophoria. Moreover, we know that the Neolithic Age is defined by the advent of agriculture, for which early women's expertise in plants is credited.[130] In direct conflict with the gender oppression in the everyday lives of women in ancient Greece, the rituals at the Thesmophoria encouraged them to celebrate the multi-faceted reproductive powers of their femininity.

The Primary Source

But how do we know what transpired at the Thesmophoria? After all, the rituals were considered

129   Burkett, 244-245.
130   Erica Simon, *Festivals of Attica; An Archaeological Commentary* (Madison, Wisconsin: University of Wisconsin Press, 1983), 17.

women's mysteries and as such, were secret and known only to its female participants. The oldest and best source of the rituals conducted in the Thesmophoria are marginal notes (scholia) by a medieval scribe found in a thirteenth-century manuscript titled Lucian's (125 CE-180 CE) *Dialogues of the Courtesans*.

Ancient scholia are important sources of information about many aspects of the ancient world and are often found in the margins of manuscripts written by ancient authors. Usually they are anonymous with the earliest of them dating back to the fifth or fourth century BCE. The narrative the scholiast used in describing the Thesmophoria's rites is from the Orphic version of the *Hymn to Demeter*. Because the Orphic version came later than the *Hymn* (third to second century BCE as opposed to the *Hymn's* seventh century BCE), new characters had been added to the myth. Under this version of events, upon Persephone's abduction, an unfortunate swineherd (Eubouleus) and his pigs are swallowed into the chasm when the earth cleaves open. The scholiast writes:

> *The rotted remains of those things which have been thrown into the chambers below are brought up by women called bailers who after having purified themselves for three days, descend into the innermost sanctuaries and carrying them up, lay them on the altars. They believe that anyone*

who takes them and mixes them with seed will have abundant crops.[131]

The text produced by the Lucian scholiast was initially published in 1870 by Erwin Rohde, one of the great classical scholars of the nineteenth century, not long before Frazer wrote *The Golden Bough* in 1890. Some think that the Lucian scholiast may have deeply influenced Frazer's thinking on "agrarian magic," for which he would become renowned.[132]

There have been a number of theories as to whom the scholiast may have been. Rohde attributed the writings to Didymus (63 BCE- 10 CE), a prolific ancient Greek scholar and grammarian responsible for penning thirty-five hundred treatises. Another name that emerges was the first century BCE Greek scholar, Apollodorus of Athens in his discourse on festivals. Finally, the fourth century BCE philosopher and pupil of Aristotle, Theophrastus, has recently been named as the possible scholiast.

But a question that has dogged each of these claims is how would any of these men have had access to the closely guarded women's rites? After translating the document, classicist Nicholas Lowe examined the work done by the above contenders and one by one convincingly eliminates the possibility that any of these

---

131   Scholiast to Lucian quoted in Stallsmith, 3.
132   Lowe, 149.

men could be the scholiast. In fact, Lowe speculates that the author of this *"surprisingly sophisticated model"*[133] must have been an actor in the ritual herself. Although he does not come right out and say it—the presumption is that the scholiast may have been a female participant. After all, only women were its actors. Who else but a citizen-wife participant would know the account with such detail? More importantly, the very reason for the rites is spelled out: *"They believe that anyone who takes them and mixes them with the seed will have abundant crops."*[134] After being buried for eons, could the Lucian scholiast have been the voice of a citizen-wife herself returning from her primordial domain to indoctrinate us on the Thesmophoria's cryptic rites?

---

133   Lowe,156.
134   Stallsmith, 4.

1. Marble Figure of Demeter of Knidos c. 350-330 BCE

2. The Peplos Kore c. 530 BCE

3. Zeus of Athens (Artemision Bronze) c. 200 CE

4. Hades and Cerberus Mid 2nd century CE,
Heraklion Archaeological Museum

5. Rape of Persephone (Apulian Red-Figure Volute-Krater) c. 340 BCE

6. Demeter Scolding Metaneira (Apulian Red-Figure Hydra) c. 340 BCE

7. The Ascension of Persephone from the Underworld
by "Persephone Painter" c440 BCE

8. Demeter Drives Horse-Drawn Chariot
with Persephone (Selinunte, Sicily)
C. 6th Century BCE

9. Double Goddesses of Catal Huyuk c. 6000 BCE

10. Photo of Sanctuary of Demeter in Corinth

11. The Pnyx Plateau---Athens present day

12. Photo of Areopagus---Athens Present Day

13. Demeter and Persephone with Mushroom from
Temple Wall at Eleusis c. 4th century BCE

14. Figurine of Demeter with Pig Athens c. 5th century BCE

15. Terracotta Pig Statuette from Boeotia c. 5th century BCE

16. Seated Mother Goddess of Catal Huyuk c. 6000 BCE

17. The Daughters of Danaus. by Fernand Sabatte c. 1900

18. A Portion of the Telesterion in Eleusis---Present day

19. Eleusinian Trio, Persephone, Triptolemus, and Demeter
Marble bas-relief from Eleusis c. 440-430 BCE

20. Eleusinian Mysteries Hydria showing reunion of the
twin goddesses, red-figure hydria c. 4th century BCE

21. Red-figure lecythus showing a young woman
throwing piglet into megaron c. 5th century BCE

22. A Greek Terracotta Female Votary Holding
a Piglet (Sicily) c. 5th century BCE

23. Apulian bell-krater illustrating scene from
Thesmophoriazusae c. 370 BCE

CHAPTER THREE

THE PREHISTORIC ORIGINS
OF THE THESMOPHORIA

D elving into the origins of the Thesmophoria is essential to determine its prehistoric significance in the devotional lives of the early disciples. It also provides insight into the meaning the primordial festival had for subsequent generations. But first, what did the term "Thesmophoria" mean to the early followers? As is often the case with this prehistoric women's festival, there is more than one possible explanation for the name.

The simple answer is that *thesmoi* in Greek means law. One of Demeter's titles is *Thesmophoros*, which translates into lawgiver. Why is Demeter, who is associated with agriculture, linked to law? In point of fact, the average Greek associated agriculture with civilization, because if it were not for the ability to grow crops, the early Greeks would never have settled as a people. The eminent classicist, Fritz Graf declared, "*Demeter is not just responsible for the gift of corn*[135] *(i.e., grains) but for the rise of civilization it entails.*"[136] Once the early Greeks developed agriculture, they evolved from roaming nomads that had no organized laws to farmers living in a community; hence the laws were necessary for the ability to work together as one society.

Some scholars, however, take exception to this narrow definition of the term "Thesmophoria," and suggest instead that *thesmoi* also meant "*the things laid down.*" In relation to the festival, it refers to the sacred objects, which were scooped from the cavern and laid down on the altar before the goddesses as an offering for a successful harvest. Harrison observes: "*The women were called Thesmophoroi because they carried 'the things laid down;' the goddess took her name from her ministrants.*"[137] After all, the laying down of the consecrated items to the goddesses was integral to the very justification behind the rites.

---

135   The term "corn" is used repeatedly in this book as the grain for which Demeter is known. However the grain for which Demeter was responsible, was in fact wheat. The early archaeologists and classicists were primarily British (or influenced by British English) and they used the terms "corn" and "wheat" interchangeably.

136   Fritz Graf "Eleusis und die orphische Dichtung Athens im vorbellenisteischer Zeit" quoted in Lowe, 154.

137   Harrison, 137.

Burkert concurs, adding that it was when these items were carried from the pits to the altars: *"....that the name of the festival is to be understood."*[138] Many experts agree that the term "things laid down" is inherent in the name of the festival, because the suffix *phoria* indicates "items carried", which signifies physical objects.[139]

While the suffix *can* work with the root "laws" such as in the phrase "carrying ordinances" that was probably not the case. Laws are non-material items and in Greek—unlike in English—attaching a non-material item to a material one forms an abnormal word combination.[140] Depending upon the time frame, however, both definitions can be accurate. In post-Homeric Greek literature—which was during the Archaic era—the *thesmoi* was written to reflect the notion of laws, which helps explain why Demeter is associated as the law-giving goddess. But sequentially not only does the Thesmophoria festival precede Homeric literature, more importantly, it also precedes the medium of writing itself and the establishment of laws by perhaps thousands of years. Hence the original disciples of the Thesmophoria would have likely defined their festival not by the laws

---

138   Burkert, 243.

139   Simon, 19.

140   H. W. Parke, *Festivals of the Athenians*, (London: Thames and Hudson Ltd., 1977), 83.

for which they would have had no knowledge, but by the sacred objects for which their cult was noted.[141]

Swine and Wheat

Relevant to this, how did objects become sacred during prehistoric times? According to archaeological and literary sources, the Thesmophoria had its origins in the Neolithic era (ca 6800 BCE-3200 BCE) when agriculture and swine domestication began concurrently. In the Mediterranean, pigs (see Figure 15) are believed to have been one of the first animals to be domesticated during the agricultural revolution, leading renowned anthropologist Marija Gimbutas to assert that:

> The fast-growing body of the pig will have been compared to corn growing and ripening, so that its soft fats apparently came to symbolize the earth itself, causing the pig to become a sacred animal probably no later than 6000 BC.[142] [143]

141   Simon, 19.

142   Marija Gimbutas. *The Goddess and Gods of Old Europe: Myths & Cult Images*, (Berkeley: University of California Press, 1982), 211.

143   In the 1990's there was an effort to discredit the work of the archaeologist, Gimbutas, however since that time her scholarship has been affirmed. Author and cultural historian Charlene Spretnak writes: "Her Kurgan theory of how, where, and when the Indo-European nomadic tribes migrated into Eastern Europe has now been been proved by historical genome mapping."

Because of this juxtaposition, the primeval populace saw a correlation between the flourishing of both livestock (swine) and crops such as wheat, demonstrating to them that the two processes were inexplicably related. Indubitably, human and crop fertility were major concerns for the Neolithic population. Thus, in order to conjure a successful harvest that ensured the health and well-being of the populace, a link between hogs and crops, as demonstrated in the Thesmophoria, became inevitable. In discussing Neolithic artifacts related to the Thesmophoria, Burkert posits:

> *Pig sacrifices are a special feature of these festivals, and terracotta votive pigs are frequently found in Demeter shrines. An impressive clay pig figure, once again dating from the Early Neolithic has been uncovered; the clay pigs studded with grains of corn, which have been found in the Balkans, make their connection with agriculture immediately apparent.* [144]

Owing to gender roles not being finely demarcated as they would in subsequent eras, agriculture and hog domestication began concurrently and both were the domain of women in the Neolithic era in the Greek

---

144   Burkert, 13.

world.[145] While men were on one hunting expedition after another, women stayed behind foraging for plants. It was foraging that gave women expertise in vegetation. Eventually, this expertise led to the cultivation of seeds which produced the plants that would go on to become humankind's principal foods.

Contemporaneous to cultivating the land, the raising of livestock (in the form of swine) allowed a previously nomadic people to settle the land. Archaeologists attest that women played critical roles during this time; they were in charge not only of breeding the population but of feeding it as well.

"*Here it was the women who showed themselves supreme,*" observes German philosopher, Wilhelm Schmidt, "*By realizing that it was possible to cultivate, as well as gather, they had made the earth valuable and they became, consequently, its possessors,*"[146]

As archaeological artifacts from the region attest, women were revered in the Neolithic age (see Figure 16), playing a dominant role in the fertility of human, livestock, and plant life. In point of fact, anthropomorphic statuary in late Neolithic Crete were four times as

145 Simon, 17; Mara Lynn Keller, "The Eleusinian Mysteries of Demeter and Persephone," *Journal of Feminist Studies in Religion* 4, no. 1 (Spring 1988); Merlin Stone, *When God Was a Woman*, (Orlando, FL: Harcourt Inc, 1976), 14.

146 Wilhelm Schmidt quoted in Joseph Campbell, *Primitive Mythology* (New York: Penguin Group, 1969), 320.

likely to be female than male.[147] While matriarchal rule is largely speculative, most scholars concur that the social structure was either matrifocal or matrilineal, meaning that mothers were the head of the household and kinship was assumed through the maternal line. As touched upon in a previous chapter, patriarchal marriage did not exist during the Neolithic era.[148]

The Mother-Daughter Relationship

During this time mother and mother-daughter images (see Figure 9) are found throughout old Europe, while the father figure is largely missing. In the words of Marija Gimbutas, *"The role of father in prehistoric antiquity was either not fully understood or not as highly valued as that of mother."*[149] When the Thesmophoria originated, the notion of paternity may not have been fully comprehended and thus the festival was about women's role in fertility without the male agent. To be sure, not only is maternity easier to detect, but it is also more verifiable than paternity. In a society that does not mate for life and assumes its ancestry through maternal lines, knowledge of paternity was not only incomprehensible, but possibly also not necessary.

---

147   Pomeroy, 14-15.
148   Likely, patriarchal marriage did not exist during much of the Greek Bronze age (3200-1200) either.
149   Marija Gimbutas, *The Living Goddesses* (Berkeley, CA: University of California Press, 2001), 112.

Their ignorance of paternity has led many to believe that in the prehistoric era, the female body was believed to be parthenogenetic. In other words, the female body was understood to create life from within itself, with no male intervention.[150] If paternity was not comprehended during this time, then the notion of female-only birth must have been credible. Doubtless, paternity would have become better understood with the raising of livestock.[151]

While women may or may not have practiced parthenogenesis in the prehistoric Greek world, doubtless their divinities did.[152] Rigoglioso proposes that the Thesmophoria was originally a parthenogenesis celebrating ritual with Persephone set to play the role of a parthenogenetic goddess before being violated by a patriarchal god.[153] According to the theory, it was not only Persephone who was parthenogenetic, Demeter

---

150   Gimbutas, 112; Rigoglioso, 100.

151   Ehrenberg, 63-65.

152   In *Theogony,* Hesiod reports that five goddesses reproduced parthenogenetically: Chaos, Gaea, Night, Strife, and Hera.

153   Rigoglioso,100-189. As examined in the first chapter on mythology, the gods of the Mycenaenean invaders raped or married the indigenous goddesses, replacing matricentric elements with patriarchal ones.

was as well.[154] In fact, a parthenogenetic Demeter may help explain why the goddesses resemble each other so strongly in artwork (see Figures 8 and 13).

Furthermore, Demeter's parthenogenesis could give fresh insight into her cryptic comment from the *Hymn*: *"the girl I bore, a sweet offshoot noble in form."*[155] Pursuant to this, it is theorized that the founding members of the Thesmophoria were celebrating feminine parthenogenesis, not only for the double goddesses but for themselves. Representing the mother/daughter bond, the lives of Demeter and Persephone oftentimes ran parallel to the lives of their adherents. That being the case, if parthenogenesis was practiced by the immortals, it might have been attempted by the mortals as well. Moreover, while the concept of parthenogenesis may seem implausible to modern sensibilities, in the mindset of the ancients, the realms between mortal and immortal often intermingled, particularly through the magic of ritual.

---

154 Ibid, 1-13. In addition to Demeter and Persephone, Rigoglioso argues that Hera, Artemis, and Athena were once parthenogenetic goddesses before being assimilated into subordinate positions (wife, sister, daughter) under patriarchal pantheons.

155 Foley, 4: line 66.

The Descent of Women

What then accounts for the twilight of the matriarch from its apex in the Neolithic era? Some believe that the answer to that question can be found in the *Hymn* itself. According to the theory, because it was an act of aggression against a goddess, Persephone's rape indicated an end to matriarchy, while ushering in an era of patriarchy where kidnapping-cum-marriage was routine.[156] *"In the immortal realms as well as the earthly plane"*, Rigoglioso posits, "*it signaled the usurping of the parthenogenetic power of the female in service to the birthing of the "'sons of gods.'"* [157] The rape/marriage motif is seen over and over again in Greek mythology when the long arm of the patriarchs squashed the parthenogenetic mother goddesses in favor of their male deities. In the second millennium, based on archaeological artifacts and epigraphic evidence, not only did the Indo-European/Mycenaean invaders bring their patriarchal war-like culture with them to the Greek mainland, they supplanted the indigenous mother goddess with thunderous sky gods and carried with them their custom of virilocal or patrilocal marriage, which they had been practicing for some time.[158] This is

---

156   Rigoglioso, 100.

157   Ibid, 100.

158   L. Fortunato, "Reconstructing the History of Marriage Strategies in Indo-European Speaking Societies: Monogamy and Polygyny," *Human Biology*, 1 no. 83 (Feb, 2011): 87-105.

aptly demonstrated by the mythical first king of Athens, Cecrops, who was credited for founding Athens in 1580 BCE and *"for making Zeus highest."*[159] But perhaps more significantly, Cecrops established the institution of patriarchal marriage and with one fell swoop brought an end to matrilineage.[160]

Greek Philosopher, Clearchos of Soli—a pupil of Aristotle informs: *"In Athens, Cecrops was the first to join one woman to one man....before this day people did not know who their fathers were."* [161]

From the beginning, as a means of restraining the autonomy of women, the patriarchs conceived of marriage as a form of ownership. By making man head of the household, a system of patrilineal succession was created, thus not only was a woman owned by her husband, but more importantly, her offspring was as well.[162] Within patriliny, men consolidated their authority by having sexual monopoly over their wives and economic and legal authority over her children. All at once, the institution of patriarchal marriage wrested matrilineal power from the hands of the matriarchs, thereby subordinating women economically, politically, and sexually. Moreover, the patriarchs deemed marriage essential for upholding society thus considered part

---

159   Pausanias quoted in Keller, 46.

160   Keller, 46.

161   Harrison, 262.

162   Ehrenberg, 64.

and parcel of civilization itself. Thereafter, stories that contradicted its advantages were deemed seditious and subversive.

The Danaids

Is it any wonder then, that the legendary founding members of the Thesmophoria were a band of sisters who did nothing to conceal their contempt for the patriarchal bond of marriage? Irrevocably forced into marriages with their cousins, forty-nine of King Danaus' fifty daughters—the Danaids—murdered their husbands on their wedding night. The earliest extant literary reference for the Thesmophoria alludes to these notorious daughters of Danaus and comes from the so-called "father of history," ancient Greek historian Herodotus (484 BCE - 425 BCE):

> About the ritual of Demeter that the Greeks call the Thesmophoria, let me keep a pious silence, except for how much of the ritual can be piously told, The daughters of Danaus were the ones who brought the ritual from Egypt and taught the Pelasgian (Greek) women.[163]

---

163 Herodotus, *The Histories* ed. A.D. Godley (2.171.2-3) http://www.perseus.tufts.edu/hopper/text?doc=Hdt.%20 2.171&lang=original.

The legend has the sisters fleeing from Egypt to Greece and setting up the sacred rites of the Thesmophoria upon their arrival. The most thorough version of the myth comes from *Bibliotheca* written by Apollodorus of Athens[164](second century BCE) and begins when a quarrel erupts between twin brothers, Egypt's King Aegyptus and Libya's King Danaus. In an effort to heal the rift, Aegyptus proposes a mass marriage between his fifty sons and the fifty daughters of Danaus. Distrustful of his brother's motives, Danaus consults an oracle who confirms his worst fears: Aegyptus plans to kill his daughters so upon marriage his sons can take their dowries. In the bones of this myth about matrimony, it is as if the daughters were Athena-like springing full-grown out of Danaus's head— one seldom hears of a mother. As is demonstrated in the *Hymn*, arranging marriages is the domain of the father. Ultimately, Danaus and his daughters sought refuge in their ancestral homeland of Argos—a principal Mycenaean citadel located in the Peloponnese.

Once the Danaids are in Argos, they discover it is suffering from the ravages of drought which as water diviners they attempt to correct. The divination works,

---

164   Apollodorus, *The Library of Greek Mythology* tr. Robin Hard. (Oxford: Oxford University Press, 1997), 60-62; Campbell Bonner, "The Danaid Myth," *Transactions and Proceedings of the American Philological Association* 31(1900) 28-36.

the kingdom is saved, and Danaus is made king of Argos.

Meanwhile, not so easily dissuaded, the fifty sons of Aegyptus insist upon wedded bliss with their reluctant cousins. Rebuffed yet again, the obdurate men lay siege on Argos. To lift the siege, Danaus must acquiesce to the wedding between his daughters and Aegyptus's sons. But unbeknownst to the obstinate cousins, Danaus equips his daughters with daggers to use on their bridegrooms as they lay sleeping. Forty-nine of the fifty blushing brides comply by beheading their husbands on their wedding night while the men lay sleeping.[165]

Ostensibly, since he respected her virginity, Hypermnestra spared the dagger with her husband, Lynceus. Her act of mercy, however, ignited the ire of Danaus who had her imprisoned. Eventually, Lynceus would rescue Hypermnestra by slaying Danaus in order to become king. With a loyal wife by his side, the legendary couple would go on to become the founding ancestors of a long line of Argive kings and heroes. Theoretically, unless parthenogenesis was involved, how they procreated while she retained her virginity is a mystery of the ages. The other forty-nine daughters buried the heads of their husbands at Lerna—an area of

---

165   Rigoglioso claims that beheading may be a euphemism for castration, 129.

springs south of Argos, where they conducted funeral rites that purified them of the murders.

In another tradition, for their troubles, the Danaids find themselves in Tartarus: the deepest, darkest, and dreariest part of Hades. Hell-like, it is confined only for enemies of the gods who are given a futile task to perform in perpetuity. Because he tried tricking the gods, it is here that Sisyphus can be found, endlessly rolling a falling boulder uphill. But the Danaids are not enemies of the gods, yet even so, they are condemned ceaselessly to carry water in sieves (leaky vessels) for eternity (see Figure 17). Harrison posits that the Danaids' punishment was unusually severe, not because they murdered their mortal husbands, but because they rejected marriage which constituted a threat to patriarchy.[166] Worth noting, although no more than a fool's errand, an ancient method of testing virginity was for women to carry water in a sieve.[167]

Drawing from the myth of the Danaids, the playwright Aeschylus (525 BCE-456 BCE) wrote his last trilogy on the errant band of sisters, often referred to as the *Danaid Tetralogy,* of which only the first play titled *The Suppliants* is extant. In *The Suppliants,* the Danaids play the eponymous characters seeking asylum in Argos from their persecuting cousins, the Egyptians. Argos

---

166   Harrison, 621.

167   Ibid, 622.

was selected as a sanctuary because Io, the Danaids' ancestress, was an Argive princess. The play begins when the Danaids throw themselves at the mercy of the King of Argos (Pelasgus) and its citizens to protect them from the unwanted marriages with their Egyptian cousins.

The intransigence of the Danaids is aptly demonstrated when they threaten to pollute Argos by hanging themselves from the statuary if they are not granted sanctuary. "*As soon as we can, from these gods, we'll hang ourselves.*"[168] Eventually, both Pelagius and the Argive citizens agree to give asylum to the Danaids. Yet despite the refuge, the Argives ready themselves for war against the Egyptians who have come to their shores expecting the Danaids to board their boats back to Egypt: "*Hasten to the boats fast as you are able, lest torn and pricked, pricked and scratched you'll be, bloody and bloodstained your heads cut off!* [169]

As king of a sanctuary city, Pelasgus defends the women from their cousins: "*These women, if they were willing, you'd be welcome to take them with you, provided that pious speech persuaded them: but not against their will.*"[170] Although it was not unusual for brides to be taken

---

168   Aeschylus, *The Suppliant Maidens*, tr. David Greene and Richard Lattimore (Chicago & London: The University of Chicago Press, 2013), line 465.

169   Ibid, lines 835-41.

170   Ibid, lines 939-41.

against their will in marriage, in the case of the Danaids, the all-important father is as unwilling as his reluctant daughters to proceed with the nuptials. Likely, a full-scale war between the two factions would be taken up in the following play of the trilogy.

Although the ending for the *Danaid* tetralogy is lost, it is believed to have followed the same pattern as Aeschylus' *Oresteia* trilogy: division, violence, then reconciliation in the establishment of a time-honored tradition. In the final play in *Oresteia*, the Court of Areopagus is founded to help pass judgment in murder trials. Similarly, in the *Danaid* trilogy, many scholars contend that in the final play the Thesmophoria festival was founded as a means of conciliation from the patriarchs to women for their compliance in patriarchal marriage. In this sense, the Thesmophoria festival was viewed as a gift bestowed on citizen-wives from male citizens for submitting to marriage, thus upholding a patriarchal cornerstone of civilization.

The Men's Interest

As renowned twentieth-century classicist George Thomson contends: "*The women were reconciled to their changed status by the foundation of a festival in which they enjoyed exclusive rights.*"[171] That the tetralogy would end with reconciliation between the sexes by the formation of the Thesmophoria is not surprising; the Thesmophoria proved comforting not only for citizen-wives, but for male citizens as well, since it was a festival commemorating the absence of ancient violence in future marriages *"by the production of properly successful wives."*[172]

Female violence was a palpable threat to the success of the patriarchate, in that sense, men had as much to gain from the feminine fertility festival as women. Observing a time in the old matriarchal order, Harrison contends that men's support of the Thesmophoria was not unlike a Neolithic male making peace with the community in return for exclusive privileges with a particular woman.[173]

A vital question when analyzing the play is why were the Danaids fervently opposed to marriage? Did they resist the institution of marriage itself or was it incestual marriage to their cousins in particular? To answer these questions it is important to have an understanding of Greek law. In much of the Greek world, there were no laws against marriage with first cousins.

---

171 George Thomson, *Aeschylus and Athens: The Classic Study in the Social Origins of Drama* (New York: Grosset & Dunlap, 1968), 295-296.

172 Goff, 137-138.

173 Harrison, 131.

In fact, far from a law barring such a union, the laws of inheritance actually encouraged it. In Athens, if a father died leaving only daughters, the daughters would have been claimed by the next male kin—his brothers or their sons.

The truth is, the reason the cousins passionately pursued the Danaids was not so much sentimental as it was pecuniary—the cousins desired not their persons but their substantial dowries. In the play, when asked by Pelasgus why they have come to Argos, the Danaid chorus leader replies: "*So as not to be a slave to Egyptus' sons.*"[174] Then in a veiled reference to incest as the possible cause for the Danaids' aversion to the marriages, Pelasgus asks "*Is this from hatred, or does the law forbid it*?"[175] Disavowing that incest is the reason—after all, marriage between royal family members was de rigueur in Egypt—a Danaid replies "*What woman could like a man she buys as her owner?*"[176]

In Euripides' *Medea,* Medea makes a similar lament: "*First, you have to pay an enormous sum to buy a husband who, to make things worse, gets to be master of your body.*"[177] Not only did marriage shackle a woman in bondage, but she was meant to pay for the privilege.

---

174   Aeschylus, line 335.
175   Ibid, line 336.
176   Ibid, line 337.
177   Euripides, *Medea,* tr. Sheila Murnaghan, (New York, London: W. W. Norton & Company, 2018), line 214.

Because they valued their freedom above all else, the Danaids were resolutely opposed to marriage—much like the early matriarchs of whom they refer: *"We, the great seed of a Holy mother, ah me! Grant us that we unwed, unsubdued, from marriage of men may flee."*[178]

In fact, the Danaids' aversion to marriage is matched in magnitude by the perseverance of their cousins who would have them as wives against their wills. The subtext of the tale is women's fear of losing autonomy on the one hand, and the threat of violence against them on the other. In the tradition of the powerful Amazons, who they more than a little resembled, the Danaids hearken back to a time when women overtly opposed the yoke of marriage.

Opposition to Marriage

The earliest myth about feminine opposition to marriage, the *Hymn* supplies the narrative of marriage as a violent abduction or rape. Revealing a profound hostility to marriage, many scholars see a symmetry between the *Hymn* and the myth of the Danaids. In a blatant display of male hegemony, the cousins—like Hades before them—forcefully inflict marriage, that is sanctioned rape, on the unwilling brides. Playing the double roles of Persephone as a reluctant wife and

---

178   Aeschylus, line 140.

Demeter as a fierce and vengeful matriarch, the actions of the Danaids are as singular and violent as those of the double goddesses. In both myths, the dark bargain made by the males is a misbegotten one; the earth is transformed into a barren wasteland by the wrath of Demeter in the *Hymn*, while beheading awaits the forty-nine bridegrooms by their furious brides in the myth of the Danaids.

The symmetry, however, goes even deeper. Beckoning from the fertile-rich Nile, the Danaids were known as well-nymphs, and as such, acted as water-diviners to the water-starved Argives bringing them the life-saving gift of irrigation. Throughout the Greek world, water was an elusive but essential element to agricultural success, hence a complementary component to Demeter's role as fertility goddess.

In light of the similarities between the two myths, Herodotus rightfully apprehended the link between the Danaids and the cult festival of the Thesmophoria, each with its own distinct aversion to matrimony. Although the story of the Danaids is considered an Argive foundational myth, like many myths, ancient and modern historians alike have argued that the legend has a historical basis. Besides Herodotus, some ancients who were known to have referred to the Danaids as historical characters include: Plato (428-348 BCE), Diodorus Siculus (90 BCE-30 BCE), and Strabo (64 BCE-21 CE).[179] More recently,

179   Harrison. 614.

20th-century classicist A. B. Cook identified a link between a historical Greco-Libyan tribe known as the Daanau, who attacked the Kingdom of Ramses of Egypt in 1200 BCE to Homer's Danaans from the *Iliad,* who are referenced time and time again in the epic.[180] Moreover, their eponym, Danaos, would have been discernible by Greeks as coming from Egypt. In referencing the mainland Greeks, Homer uses the collective names of Achaeans, Argives, and Danaans interchangeably.[181]

Lastly, in his seminal and at times controversial book about ancient Greece's Afroasiatic roots, *Black Athena*, based on linguistic and archaeological evidence, Martin Bernal argues that the Danaids were historical figures from the Bronze Age.[182] Like the myth, the Danaids were involved in a battle for power in Egypt against male adversaries, whom they ultimately killed before fleeing to Argos and settling there.

The Greek-Egyptian Connection

But aside from the possibility of the Danaids being historical, many believe there was a strong link between

---

180   Arthur Bernard Cook, *Zeus: A Study in Ancient Religion* (Cambridge: Cambridge University Press, 2015.

181   Homer never called himself Greek. Greeks referred to themselves as Hellenes and to their country as Hellas. The terms "Greeks" and "Greece" are Latin and how the Romans referred to their neighbors to the east.

182   Martin Bernal, *Black Athena:The Afroasiatic Roots of Classical Civilization* (London: Vintage Books, 1991).

Egypt and Greece going back to the very beginning of the Mycenaean culture during the second-millennium BCE—an era when ancient Egypt was at its peak. Could Egypt have colonized parts of the Greek world as Herodotus argued?

In the words of Herodotus, "*How it happened that Egyptians came to the Peloponnese, and what they did to make themselves kings in that part of Greece, has been chronicled by other writers.*" [183]

Alas, the chronicles Herodotus refers to are lost to posterity. Herodotus, however, is not the only ancient who draws a deep connection between the two civilizations. In his dialogue *Timaeus,* Plato infers an ancient "genetic" link between Egypt and Greece.[184] Fascinating as this is, to date, no such genetic link has been established.

Finally, even Plutarch (50 CE- 120 CE) in *Isis and Osiris* draws a connection between the two civilizations when he apprehends a relationship between the primordial Thesmophoria and the cult of Isis in Egypt.[185] To be sure, as divine earth mothers, there are strong parallels between Isis and the goddess of the harvest,

183   Herodotus, *Histories* VI.55.
184   Bernal, 22.
185   Plutarch, *Moralia*, vol V (Loeb Classical Library: 1936). https://penelope.uchicago.edu/Thayer/e/roman/texts/plutarch/moralia/isis_and_osiris*/b.html.

Demeter. In fact, Demeter descends from the matriarchal tradition of which Isis was an archetype.

Through the ages, because of rich cultural symmetries between the two civilizations, historians have espoused a foundational connection between Egypt and parts of the Greek world. Although such links remain unverified other links are clear. Based on archaeological evidence both Greek antecedents— the Minoan and Mycenaean civilizations—traded extensively with Egypt. Although tangibles such as copper and gold were actively traded, likely non-tangibles such as mythology and religion were exchanged as vigorously. Moreover, by the sixth century BCE, robust trade routes between ancient Greece and Egypt were routine. Little is certain in looking back over a span of four thousand years, except for this: the contributions of Egypt on the culture of ancient Greece are, regrettably, oftentimes overlooked.

CHAPTER FOUR

THE ELEUSINIAN MYSTERIES

Demeter's Rites of Eleusis better known as the Eleusinian Mysteries were noteworthy by their egalitarianism on the one hand and their exclusivity on the other. It was open to everyone—male and female alike as long as they were free of "bloodguilt" (murder) but exclusive only to those who were initiated into their secret rites. Unlike most religious festivals which were available to the public and celebrated during the day, the Eleusinian Mysteries (hereafter called the Mysteries) were noteworthy by their singularity; open only to initiates with rites clandestinely held in the dead of the night. Considered the most acclaimed of all religious festivals throughout the Greek world, like the Thesmophoria, the Mysteries honored Demeter, goddess of the harvest, and her daughter, Persephone, queen of the underworld. Although agriculture played a part in the rites, its role would become greatly diminished in favor of the eschatological nature of Demeter's story; that is issues regarding life after death. In the minds of the ancients, nature's resurrection was emblematic of humankind's immortality.

But in a book about an exclusive woman's-only fertility festival, why is there a chapter on a secret cult known for its comparative inclusiveness? The largest and most renowned of all mystery or secret cults, many argue that the famed Eleusinian Mysteries sprang forth as a male response to the Thesmophoria. In view of the fact that more has been written about the Mysteries than the Thesmophoria, a comprehensive study about the cult may prove enlightening to apprehending its older sister. Secret initiation rites held under cover of darkness, rumors of spectacular pyrotechnics, and the buoyant promise of immortality— the Mysteries conjure up cabalistic images of a dark and dangerous festival. In fact, it was surrounded by such an aura of deadly secrecy that the tragedian Aeschylus (525 BCE- 455 BCE) was nearly killed on stage just for referencing it. But for all that has been written about the Mysteries over the ages, what were they really about? And how did they differ from their older sister, the Thesmophoria?

Thought to have predated the Greek Dark Ages (1100 BCE-800 BCE), the Mysteries reach back into the Mycenaean era (1600 BCE- 1100 BCE) while the bulk of evidence about the festival dates from the Archaic era (800 BCE- 480 BCE) of ancient Greece.[186] Although its foundations were in the Greek world, they were celebrated throughout the Roman Empire up until 389 CE and garnered near-universal reverence up until the late fourth century CE when Byzantine Emperor Theodosius I put forth an edict forbidding the worship of any deities, but the Christian father and son.[187] But the Mysteries—more than a religious festival—would become a civic festival where its renown in ancient Greece and beyond played a pivotal role in the region's concept of "cultural hegemony."[188]

Why so Mysterious?

What, then, was so mysterious about the Eleusinian Mysteries? The answer can be found in the name itself. The novice initiates of the cult were called *mystai (*singular-*mystes)* and the accompanying ever-secret initiation ritual was called *mysteria*. Hence the Mysteries were a secret cult whose participation was restricted to its initiates wherein initiation ceremonies played a key role in the sacred rituals. The truth is the

---

186   Foley, 171.

187   Nancy A. Evans, Sanctuaries, Sacrifices and Eleusinian Mysteries, *Numen,* 49, no. 3 (2002), 230-231. https://www.jstor.com/stable/3270542.

188   Kevin Clinton, *Myth and Cult: The Iconography of the Eleusinian Mysteries* (Stockholm:Svenksa Institute I Athens), 1990, 32.

secrecy around the cult added to its aura. *"The silence that was preserved as to the ceremonies and sacred symbols constituted a halo which added considerably to the awe that surrounded the Mysteries,"*[189] contends Classical scholar Paul Carus, lamenting that the secrecy with which it was practiced greatly reduces the amount of information that is available for study.

But perhaps it was its aura of secrecy that has compelled historians throughout the ages to study the elusive Mysteries. They were composed of both the Lesser Mysteries which honored Persephone and were observed in the spring and the Greater Mysteries, honoring Demeter and celebrated six months later in the month of Boedromion, now known as September-October. This was directly before the sowing season, which heralded the Thesmophoria. As a preparation for the Greater Mysteries, a candidate could become a *mystes* (initiate or blinded one) to begin his or her worship in the ranks of the Lesser Mysteries only to progress into the more enlightened Greater Mysteries once his or her initiation was complete. The initiation period is believed to have been a year, after which time the *mystes* would ascend into the hallowed ranks of *epoptes* (seer and hearer) and be able to participate

---

189   Paul Carus, "The Greek Mysteries, A Preparation for Christianity," *The Monist* 11, no. 1 (October 1900): 87, https://www.jstor.org/stable/27899193.

as a full initiate of the Greater or *Epoptical* "all-seeing" Mysteries.[190]

Though the most sacred of the rituals were celebrated in Eleusis—an agricultural town some fourteen miles northwest of Athens—people came from all over the Greco-Roman world into Athens to participate in the nine-day long event. The procession from Athens to Eleusis was considered the most elaborate and spectacular of all religious parades in the ancient world. In fact, the road between the two cities—-called the Sacred Way—-became so legendary that before the Romans arrived, it was the only road in all of central Greece that was not a goat path.[191] While the Thesmophoria included possibly up to a hundred local celebrations throughout the Greek world; the Mysteries had adherents from all over the Greco-Roman world but was celebrated locally—-only in Athens and Eleusis. Until the mid-sixth century BCE, Eleusis alone had control of its own cult. After it was conquered by Athens, however, the Athenians assumed control, putting the Mysteries on the map and transforming them from Demeter's Rites at Eleusis into the celebrated Eleusinian Mysteries.[192]Athens is not mentioned in the

---

190   Carus, 100.
191   Joshua J. Mark, "The Eleusinian Mysteries Rites of Demeter," https://www.worldhistory.org/article/32/the-eleusinian-mysteries-the-rites-of-demeter/.
192   Mylonas, 131; Keller, 48.

Hymn because the authoring of the narrative preceded its involvement in the rites.

Although men were irrevocably banned from the female-only Thesmophoria, their participation in the Eleusinian Mysteries was welcome. Ostensibly, membership in the Mysteries was unrestricted, open to all men and women, slaves and foreigners alike— everyone *"free of the pollution of murder"*[193] or "blood guilt" could participate. Yet, there were some restrictions. Although foreigners were welcome in the mysteries—initiates had to speak Greek. Similarly, *"not being a barbarian"* was a requirement.[194] This, however, changed when Athens assumed control of the rites and lifted the Greek-speaking requirement in order to promote the Mysteries across the Greek world and beyond.

Might they also have lifted the bloodguilt ban? Classical philosopher, Mara Lynn Keller in her paper about the Eleusinian Mysteries posits that because militarism engulfed the region, soldiers were aplenty and encouraged to join the Mysteries.[195] In the interest of Athenian hegemony, soldiers—-who presumably had blood guilt —-would have joined the Mysteries with abandon. However, despite loosening their standards for some, during the fourth-century BCE, Athens made

---

193   Evans, 240.

194   Keller, 48.

195   Ibid, 48.

a change that would make it more restrictive for others when it began requiring initiates to pay fifteen drachmas for the privilege of membership. Fifteen drachmas were equivalent to ten days labor—an amount that the poor or enslaved would likely have been unable to pay.[196]

A Change of Focus

Like the Thesmophoria, the Mysteries were associated with agriculture, but after Athens became involved in the rites the focus changed from human and plant regeneration to eternal life for cult members. This is a point in which the differences between the two cults are very apparent. While the rituals of the Thesmophoria were concerned with Demeter's imparting gifts of fertility to women and the cyclical nature of creation, the rituals enacted in the Eleusinian Mysteries tended to have more of a masculine appeal, focusing on the role immortality plays in the story.

Of the Mysteries, the poet Pindar (498 BCE - 436 BCE) opined: *"Blessed is he who has beheld the mysteries, descending in the Netherworld. He knows the aim, he knows the origin of life."*[197] To be sure, the main focus of the Mysteries was a happy afterlife, which initiates were promised through membership in the cult.

---

196   Burkert, 67-68.
197   Pindar quoted in Carus, 101.

In her article, "Ritual Death and Patriarchal Violence," Classics professor, Marcia W. D-S. Dobson contends that the difference in focus between the two cults could be based on gender, as women are closer to the cyclical patterns of nature and therefore more accepting of death. "*Because the male connection to the natural rhythms of life and death are not as immediate, a man experiences his mortality as a devastation of his individuality*."[198] Rebelling against nature, men are at odds with the periodic patterns of regeneration that the two goddesses represent, hence the assurance of a happy afterlife helps them overcome this dissonance.

Although women were more closely aligned to natural rhythms, were they any less interested in the notion of a happy afterlife than men? Or could it have been more than gender differences that played a part in the change of focus between the two festivals? It was during the Archaic era, when the Mysteries were in full swing, that the attitude toward death and afterlife began to shift.

Prior to this era, death was viewed as part of the natural order of things, thus there was a resigned acceptance of its gloomy inevitability. Over the course of time, people began disconnecting themselves

---

198   Marcia W. D-S Dobson, "Ritual Death, Patriarchal Violence, and Female Relationships in the Hymn To Demeter and Inanna," *NWSA Journal,* 4, no. 1 (Spring 1992), 49. https://www.jstor.org/stable/4316175.

from the cyclical patterns of nature, death became more personal, and greater anxiety about it ensued. Discussing changing attitudes toward death, Christiane Sourvinous-Inwood, a leading voice regarding the Hellenic world, argues about a change of mind-sets in the Archaic period:

> ....*from an acceptance of a familiar (hateful but not frightening) death to the appearance of attitudes of greater anxiety and a more individual perception of one's death, conducive to the creation of eschatologies involving a happy afterlife.*[199]

Alas, Elysian Fields awaited only those infrequent few who were bestowed with immortality by the gods. To be sure, until the Mysteries began to gain a foothold, afterlife for the ancients was a cheerless proposition. Regardless of achievements and position in life, kings and slaves alike could expect to spend eternity fluttering around endlessly in a shadowy underworld. Even Achilles, war-hero great and demigod in life, is reduced to an insubstantial shade in dusty death:

---

199   Christiane Sourvinou-Inwood, "Aspects of the Eleusinian Cult," in *Greek Mysteries: The Archaeology and Ritual of Ancient Greek Secret Cults,* ed. Michael B. Cosmopoulos (London: Routledge, 2003), 28.

No winning words about death to me, shining Odysseus! By god, I'd rather slave on earth for another man—Some dirt-poor tenant farmer who scrapes to keep alive—than rule down here over all the breathless dead.[200]

After all, if such a dismal destiny awaited a near god, what chance did an average bloke have? At the end of the day, faced with the prospect of a happy afterlife, is it any wonder that the ancients were lining up in droves to become initiates in the Eleusinian Mysteries?

From the deep recesses of the Archaic era to "enlightened" Imperial Rome, the list of initiates into the Mysteries reads like the who's who of the Classical era—indeed some of antiquity's greatest names graced their ranks, though not everyone made the cut. According to Seutonius (69 CE-122 CE), because of the bloodshed associated with his name, Nero (37 CE-68 CE) was denied membership into the popular cult.[201] Most notable ancients, however, were initiated into the Mysteries at one point or another in their lives.

---

200   Homer, *The Odyssey*, tr. Robert Fagles (New York: Penguin Putnam, 1990), 11:488-492.

201   C. Seutonius Tranquillius, *The Twelve Caesars* tr. H. M. Bird, London: Wordsworth Editions, 1997, 264, chapter 34.4:"When he was in Greece, he durst not attend the celebration of the Eleusinian mysteries, at the initiation of which, impious and wicked persons are warned by the voice of the herald from approaching the rites."

For the Record

Of course initiates would have been very reluctant to share their secrets, because it was heretical and punishable by death to do so—as well as against the law.[202] Nonetheless, if it was not for their writing, along with the less reliable accounts from tendentious Christian zealots, the rites of the Mysteries would have been lost to posterity. As it stands, because of the cult's hallmark secrecy, there is heated debate amongst the academic community as to the exact nature of the rites.

While the rites themselves may be in contention, where the rites were celebrated is not. To accommodate its great number of initiates, Demeter's Temple, also called the Telesterion or initiation hall, stood at a regal 51 x 51 meters (167 feet x 167 feet). The largest public building in the fifth century (BCE) Attica, the Telesterion (see Figure 18) was a roofed temple with seating for several thousand spectators on eight rising steps.[203] Unlike today's religious structures which are meeting places, Greek temples were usually not designed for adherents, but built solely to house deities. In this aspect, the Telesterion was a departure from conventional

202   Jakub Filonik, "Athenian Impiety Trials: A Reappraisal," *ResearchGate*, file:///Users/mary/Downloads/Athenian-impietytrialsFilonik2013Dikeerrata2015embedded.pdf, 23; Renaud Gagne, "Mystery Inquisitors: Performance, Authority and Sacrilege at Eleusis," *Classical Antiquity*, 28, no.2 (October, 2009), 211-247.
203   Evans, 235.

temples of the day; inside was its inner holy sanctum, called the Anaktoron. The Anaktoron was an interior chamber where the holiest of holy rites were performed and where the *hiera* or sacred objects were kept. Only *hierophants* were allowed access to this sacred space.

Classics professor Nancy Evans likened the Telesterion to an indoor square theater,[204] which is an apt comparison as the main event was believed to be highly theatrical. Perhaps the renown of the festival had as much to do with theatrics as with eternal salvation. In fact, some posit that the works of the early tragedians (all of whom were initiates)[205]— indeed the art of theater itself—may have sprung forth from the spectacular stagecraft presented during the Mysteries' rites.

The Holy Players

The lead actor in the *mysteria* (secret rite) was the head priest or the *hierophant* which in ancient Greek refers to the priestly displayer of holy things. Appointed to this life-long position, the *hierophant* was required to be from one of the original clans of Eleusis and it was imperative that he possess a melodious voice, since singing played a considerable role in the

---

204   Evans, 234.
205   The tragedians whose works are known to us (Aeschylus, Euripides, and Sophocles) were all initiates in the Mysteries.

rites.[206] Most likely it was the *hierophant* who acted in the role of Triptolemus—an all-important mythological, scepter-wielding youth, who appears between the two goddesses in artwork from the era (see Figure 19).[207] Though Triptolemus played a minor role as Demeter's priest in the original *Hymn*, his part was greatly enhanced in the Mysteries when he became famous for introducing both agriculture and the Eleusinian Mysteries to humankind. In some renditions of the myth, Triptolemus was a counterpart to Demophoon[208] though his story had a happier ending than that of the thwarted immortal.

Next in line to the *hierophant* was the *dadouchos* or torchbearer. This second most important priest was also a life-long appointed, as well as hereditary, position.[209] Because of his role as torchbearer, some posit that the *dadouchos* may have played the part of the cult hero, Eubouleus. Although his character is not in the *Hymn*, the hapless swineherd Eubouleus does appear in an Orphic rendition of Demeter's myth. He, along with his

206 Kevin Clinton, "Epiphany in the Eleusinian Mysteries." *Illinois Classical Studies* 29 (2004): 90, http://www.jstor.org/stable/23065342.

207 Ibid, 89.

208 Demophoon, it may be recalled, was the infant son of Metaneira who Demeter attempted to make immortal by placing in a blazing fire. Unfortunately, Demeter's efforts were foiled when Metaneira made like a mortal and screamed.

209 Ibid, 88.

swine, was sucked into a gorge when the earth cleaved open and Hades abducted Kore. Somewhere along the way, this humble swineherd informed Demeter of the whereabouts of Persephone. In fact, Eubouleus had such a cult following that in some versions of the myth, he is alternatively either the son of mighty Demeter herself or of the all-powerful Zeus.[210] Interestingly, although the Orphic version of the myth was subsequent to the *Hymn,* some contend that the Orphic myth may have reflected an even earlier tradition than the *Hymn,*[211] which may explain Eubouelus' following.

With no apparent mythological foundation, another cult figure in the Mysteries was Iacchus.[212] He is often identified with Dionysus (Bacchus) and depicted as either the son of Demeter or of Persephone and termed the "holy son." Moreover, "*Iacche*" was a ritual cry that the initiates would shout during the procession along the Sacred Way as part of the processional rite in the Mysteries.[213]

Although there were several priests below the rank of *hierophant* and the *dadouchos,* there were only three noteworthy priestesses. While one priestess

---

210   Ibid, 89.

211   Harrison, 540.

212   Keller, 49.

213   George E. Mylonas, "Eleusis and the Eleusinian Mysteries," *The Classical Journal*, 43, no.3 (Dec, 1947), 131, https// www.jstor.org/stable/3293727; Zeitlin, 309; Keller, 49; Harrison, 543.

honored the double goddesses, there were two additional priestesses called the *hierophantides;* each representing either the mother or the daughter. *Hiereiai (*singular*: hiereia)* means sacred women and was a term used for priestesses in general. According to Clinton, on the night of the *mysteria* the two *hierophantides* were said to have been decked out in full splendor to become the physical incarnations of Demeter and Persephone on earth.[214] This rite may evoke a tradition from Minoan Crete where priestesses were believed to have physically represented the great mother goddess, Ariadne. Many posit that Minoan Crete was where the Eleusinian Mysteries first originated; likewise Demeter is believed to have hailed from Minoan Crete as well.

The twin goddesses were not the only deities represented in the rites. The Mysteries emphasized the spiritual unity of all gods, as such, two important gods adopted by the Eleusinian priesthood were Dionysus and Heracles. As ancient Greek society became ever more male-oriented, the role of Dionysus as the son of Zeus began to supplant that of Persephone. Associated with fertility, Dionysus died and was resurrected each year, just like Persephone. As it happens, it may have been the presence of Dionysus and his characteristic theatrics which gave the cult its flair for drama.

---

214   Clinton, "Epiphany on the Eleusinian Mysteries," 98.

The Drama

The Mysteries were celebrated for nine days, which was the time it took for Demeter to search for Persephone while holding a torch. The drama began in Athens on the fourteenth of Boedromion (September), then made its way to the town of Eleusis on the nineteenth by way of a spectacular fourteen-mile procession along the famed Sacred Way. Amid the sounds of singing and rejoicing *(Halade, Mystae!*– to the sea, *O Mystae!)* the cacophony must have been deafening as several thousand passionate followers— initiates and non-initiates alike—-attired in festive garb came together on the packed Athenian thoroughfare for the celebrated parade.[215]

Known for its egalitarianism, all walks of life were represented at the Mysteries. From citizens to courtesans, magistrates to masons, masters and slaves alike, everyone joined the parade. After all, anyone—free of blood guilt—could be an initiate. In their full regalia, at the head of the procession, was the *hierophant,* followed by the *dadouchos,* then the priestess of the double goddesses. The two *hierophantides* representing the individual goddesses were close behind. Shadowing the sacred delegates were magistrates and *ephebes* (young men), who were responsible for escorting the *hiera* (sacred objects) to Eleusis.

---

215   Mylonas, 132.

Once in Eleusis, the *mystai* (initiates) spent the day fasting, mirroring Demeter's behavior in the *Hymn* when she was mourning for her daughter.[216] The evening of the twentieth marked the first moment the *mystai* were allowed to enter Demeter's sanctuary where the Telesterion was housed. The most sacred of all nights, known as "the scene of beholding," is believed to have been on either the twentieth or the twenty-first (or perhaps both) when the rites or *teletai* and the holy *mysteria* were performed. Once initiated, the *mystai* joined the ranks of the *epopteia* (the seeing) which was the highest degree of initiation. The initiated *epopteia* were allowed to take off their own blindfolds to behold the mysteries.

While much of what they witnessed remains under wraps, one thing is certain, fire played an enormous role in the rituals. [217]

In ancient Greece, fire was a means of communicating between the mortal and immortal realms; smoke from sacrificial fires rose to the celestial heavens as a means of placating the deity or deities for whom the sacrifice was intended. But aside from mediation between the mortal and immortal realms, fire was also used in Greek mythology as a means

---

216   In fact, the first day of the Mysteries is often compared to the all-important second day of mourning called *nesteia* in the Thesmophoria.

217   Clinton, "Epiphany on the Eleusinian Mysteries," 96.

of immortalizing humans. As mentioned previously in Chapter One, in the *Hymn*, Demeter attempts to immortalize the infant Demophoon by glazing him with ambrosia and burning him in the fire each night, "*as if he were a smoldering log.*"[218] The thinking was that because Hades stole a daughter from Demeter, she would eternalize a mortal—or, better yet, all mortals—from the lord of the underworld's thriving enterprise.[219] Of course, when Demophoon's mother, Metaniera, comes upon Demeter incinerating her son in the family hearth, she screams. This disturbs the ritual, and the mighty Demeter, incensed at the foolhardiness of mortals, tosses Demophoon to the ground. In her rage, she sentences the infant—and by implication the rest of humankind—to a life of mortal mediocrity. Thus the Eleusinian Mysteries was formed as a compensatory action to placate the anger of the goddess on the one hand, and to graciously accept her gift of immortality on the other.

While what was exactly revealed at the *mysteria* remains a mystery, based on literary and archaeological evidence, there are some theories about what may

---

218   Gregory Nagy, *Homeric Hymn to Demeter*, line 239, https://chs.harvard.edu/primary-source/homeric-hymn-to-demeter-sb/.

219   Caroline Tully, "Demeter's Wrath: How the Eleusinian Mysteries Attempted to Cheat Death" in *Memento Mori : A Collection of Magickal and Mythological Perspectives,* ed Kim Huggens (London: Avolonia, 2012), 6.

have transpired. For instance, the Mysteries were largely a visual experience; literary sources detailing the remarkable sights within the Mysteries abound, from both pagan and early Christian chroniclers. Even the names of the sacred actors in the secret cult are emblematic of this. *Hierophant* signifies "revealer of sacred objects," while the two levels of the initiates, *mystes* and *epoptes,* indicate "one whose eyes are closed" and "the seers" respectively. Of all the sights, the one that was so impressive it would remain with initiates for the rest of their lives was the phenomenal light they were to have witnessed during the sacred drama.[220] In fact, pyrotechnic expertise was characteristic of the Mysteries. In his treatise *On the Soul,* Plutarch writes:

> *But then one encounters an extraordinary light and pure regions and meadows offer welcome, with voices and dances and majesties of sacred sounds and holy sights.*[221]

This "extraordinary light" has been described by ancients before and after Plutarch as the famous "*fire at Eleusis.*"[222]

In mimesis of Demeter carrying the torch in search of Persephone, torches were widely used in the rites.

---

220   Clinton, "Epiphany"," 100.
221   Plutarch, *On the Soul* quoted in Clinton, "Epiphany," 101.
222   Clinton, "Epiphany" 100.

While principal torches were carried by the torch bearing *dadouchos* and *hierophant,* initiates carried torches as well. Clinton posits there is evidence to suggest that the extraordinary light could have come from the fire of over a thousand torches held by the initiates: *".....the extraordinary light was furnished by torchbearers—probably at least a thousand torchbearers, standing not sitting."*[223] The incandescent glow coming from so many attendees must have been spectacular. Clinton goes on to add that these torches were far more dramatic than those carried by adherents of other cults, leading to the notoriety of the fires of Eleusis. A thousand torches, however, were not the only light made reference.

The Goddesses Brought to Life

Making gods appear was another hallmark event for the Mysteries. Written in the third century CE about a *hierophant* named Apollonius, who is believed to have cried: *"O initiates, you saw me then appearing from the Anaktoron in the bright lights...."*[224] Living up to his title, it was the *hierophant's* main task to display sacred objects in the grand finale. In this case the sacred objects were the twin goddesses themselves—in all their radiant splendor. Ascending in full voice, the *hierophant* emerged from the Anaktoron in song, to reveal—in the

---

223   Ibid, 100.
224   Clinton, "Epiphany," 90.

"scene of beholding"—the colossal goddesses to the thousands in the crowd.

For the grand finale of this sacred drama, the goddesses came alive. Persephone, also known as "the Mistress of Fire," rises from the land of the dead to join Demeter in her earthly domain. At long last, mother and daughter are reunited; humankind is saved (see Figure 20). No longer just slabs of stone-cold marble. Instead, rising to celestial prominence, Demeter and Persephone looked for all the world like living goddesses. They were colorful, they were polished, but most of all, they were illuminated. It is posited that the illumination was achieved by placing fiery candles in the hollowed-out interiors of the statues.[225] By any means, the goddesses aglow by fire would have been awe-inspiring and momentous to behold.

With their blindfolds freshly removed, the thunderstruck initiate's first sight was of the glowing goddesses—indeed, such a dramatic spectacle might have rendered even the most stalwart of skeptics speechless. "*Beauty blazing out*," is how Plato describes the goddesses in *Phaedrus*.[226]

After the light festival, did the sacred actors emerge, accompanied by music and dancing to celebrate the reunion as some contend? Were hallucinogenic drugs

---

225   Clinton, "Epiphany in The Eleusinian Mysteries," 98.
226   Plato, Phaedrus, quoted in Clinton, 98.

involved in the rites as many propose? Alas, the view is often murky looking back over a span of over two thousand years. What we do know, however, is that on the following day, festivities continued and sacrifices were made in the public courtyard for the community at large. Make no mistake, this was a celebration on behalf of the entire community; even the uninitiated enjoyed the Eleusinian Mysteries.

Their revels now ended, on the twenty-third, the initiates began the journey back to Athens, concluding the nine-day long festival until the Mysteries began anew the following year. Practiced for over two thousand years, the Mysteries had become the largest and most celebrated of all religious cults in the Greco-Roman world.

Then, in 392 CE, Byzantine Emperor Theodosis I issued a comprehensive decree prohibiting pagan worship in favor of a burgeoning new religion: one that preached equality, promised a happy afterlife, and included the worship of a god whose son died and was resurrected each year so that his followers would have everlasting life. In a sense, the Mysteries live on.

CHAPTER FIVE

THE BRUTALITY OF CITIZEN-WIVES

The dominant paradigm was turned on its head when subjugated women were made autonomous by participating in the Thesmophoria. In a society where men set the rules, a community of empowered women struck fear in their hearts, and nowhere was this male fear more evident than in the stories about the brutality of the Thesmophoria's citizen-wives. The Thesmophoria was notorious for its undercurrent of ferocity towards them, because men were forbidden—-to the point of death—from attending or witnessing any portion of this all-female festival. Stories abound about men who were subject to life-threatening and disfiguring acts of violence perpetrated by the citizen-wives when they spied on or interrupted their festival in any way.

Drawn from ancient sources, some noteworthy examples of the violence of the citizen wives include the following: first, there is the tale of the legendary Messenian hero, Aristomenes (ca 720 BCE-648 BCE), who was celebrated for his triumphs against the fearsome Spartans. Unfortunately for him, he did not fare as well against the citizen-wives of the Thesmophoria. According to Pausanias (110 CE-180 CE), while in the midst of their clandestine celebration, the citizen-wives were taken hostage in Demeter's temple by Aristomenes and his fellow warriors. Hardly shrinking violets and indeed full of the mighty spirit of Demeter, the women furiously fought the errant warriors with their sacrificial knives and spits. Pausanias recounts the "mortification" of the Messenians. Imagine their humiliation, renowned for victories against the supreme Spartans, only to fall most ignominiously to the weaker sex.[227] Aristomenes himself was "knocked senseless"[228] by the hellions and only escaped with his life because of the help he received from one of Demeter's priestesses—one Arkhidameia—who, mercifully for him, happened to be his mistress.

Then there is the gruesome lore about the hapless King Battus of Cyrene (ca 650 BCE - 600 BCE), famed for founding Cyrene (Libya). In an account that sounds

---

227   Marcel Detienne, "The Violence of Wellborn Ladies: Women of the Thesmophoria," in *The Cuisine of Sacrifice Among the Greeks*, ed., Marcel Detienne and Jean-Pierre Vernant, tr.. Paula Wissing (Chicago: University of Chicago Press, 1989), 130.

228   Pausanias, 4.17.1, quoted in Detienne, 130.

suspiciously like thwarted rape, Battus threw himself at the women in the midst of their festival, refusing to budge from the sacred all-female rite. As a result of his obstinance, Battus was witness to their clandestine rites. Recounted by Claudius Aelienus (175 CE-235 CE):

> *Clothed in their holy garments, and wholly possessed because of their initiation into the mysteries, the female slayers brandished their naked swords; their hands and faces were stained with the blood of the victims.* [229]

At some point, the ceremony stopped and the women turned their attention from butchering the sacrificial pigs to butchering Battus: "*as if in response to an agreed signal, they leaped upon Battus to remove the part of him that made him a male.*"[230] Cruelly castrated by the furious disciples, the legend of King Battus is a warning to Greek men everywhere— payment is steep for violating Demeter's sacred and secret rites.

Next, there is the legend of unlucky Miltiades (555 BCE - 489 BCE), an Athenian statesman renowned for his role in the Battle of Marathon. While in a battle to secure the island of Paros, he leaped over the wall leading to the Thesmophorian shrine. Once there, he was so overcome with terror that in jumping back

---

229   Plutarch, *Nicias* 13.3-4 quoted in Detienne, 130.
230   Ibid.

over the wall he sprained his thigh,[231] from which he developed gangrene and later died.[232] Herodotus recounts this as an admonishment and warns that this mournful outcome was due to his breaching the sacred sanctuary of Demeter Thesmophoros.[233]

Finally, there is Plutarch's narrative of Pesistratus (562 BCE - 527 BCE), the tyrant of Athens, and the Athenian statesman Solon (638 BCE - 558 BCE), who pulled a trick on the women of the Thesmophoria while they were celebrating in Megara, a town ten miles from Eleusis. The famed statesmen enlisted two beardless men to impersonate the women in the sacred rites of the Thesmophoria. Ostensibly, it took no time for the enraged disciples to discover the wretched mimics and summarily attack them with their notorious knives and spits.

As violent and disfiguring as these stories may have been, they were deemed justifiable by society at large since the women of the Thesmophoria were acting on Demeter's behalf. In his influential lecture on the Greek world, Clinton maintains that regarding Plutarch's narrative above: *"Whether or not the incident is historical is for our purposes unimportant: the fact is that a celebration of the Thesmophoria at Eleusis*

---

231 By some accounts, he injured his knee.

232 Matthew Dillon, *Girls and Women in Classical Greek Religion* (London: Routledge, 2002) 110.

233 Dillon, 115.

was considered unobjectionable."[234] The narratives all demonstrate men's profound uneasiness with the female insubordination inherent in the Thesmophoria. Yet the festival was all-important to the health and prosperity of the *polis,* thus male citizens had to turn a blind eye to its subversion. Apropos to the Thesmphoria, Burkert opines: "*Men regard this not without suspicion, but cannot impede the sacred.*"[235]

A summary of stories about the violence of the citizen-wives would be incomplete without mention of Aristophanes' comedic satire *Thesmophoriazusae* or "Women at the Thesmophoria." Having fun at a fellow playwright's expense, Aristophanes casts his colleague Euripides as the character for whom the women at the Thesmophoria want revenge. "*Today at the Thesmophoria the women are going to liquidate me because I slander them,*"[236] exclaims Euripides. The premise of the play is that the rebellious disciples seek to kill Euripides for characterizing women in his plays as villainous. The women at the Thesmophoria are conducting an assembly to determine the type of punishment to mete out to the culpable Euripides, and so the playwright asks his in-law (Mnesilochus) to

234   Kevin Clinton. *Myth and Cult: The Iconography of the Eleusinian Mysteries*. (Stockholm: Svenska Institute I Athen, 1990), 29.

235   Burkert, 258.

236   Aristophanes. *Thesmophoriazusae,* tr. Alan Sommerstein (Warminister, England: Aris & Phillips, 1994), 37.

impersonate a citizen-wife so that he may influence the women in Euripides' favor. Although mocked in terms of their democratic assembly, the women are in charge while most of the men at one time or another actively impersonate them—at their peril. Gender inversion is an important theme in this comedy.[237]

Amid double entendres, there is an undercurrent of violence; Aristophanes' depiction of the women as uncontrollable and savage is in keeping with the androcentric mindset towards the festival. While the common thread in all these stories is the women's unmitigated violence against men, the patriarchy's lack of trust for the festival is similarly noteworthy. In discussing the violence associated with male interference " noted Classics professor H. S. Versnel asserts: *They (the stories) also most clearly demonstrate that the festival is essentially wrong, disruptive and consequently in the eyes of one half of society, threatening.*"[238] Drawing a primordial connection between the Thesmphorian citizen-wives and their ferocious Danaid foremothers— the forty-nine notorious sisters who slew their husbands on their wedding night—these vignettes tellingly reveal

---

237   Because Greek women were restricted from acting, gender inversion on stage was routine.

238   H.S. Versnel, "The Festival of the Bona Dea and the Thesmophoria," *Greece & Rome*, 39 (April 1992), 42. http://www.jstor.org/stable/643119.

the fear Greek men felt for the Thesmophoria and its citizen-wives.

Violence— Real or Imaginary?

Besides the subversive misandry inherent in the festival, was there something about the Thesmophoria that encouraged stories of its savagery? At this point, it is useful to review the limited rights of women in the Greek world. Wholly without agency, women were treated as children with their every move directed by a male guardian, typically in the form of husband, father, or brother. Accordingly, they were restricted from the public domain and confined to the relative seclusion of their domiciles. They were prohibited to own or inherit, even voting was forbidden in this arch-patriarchal society. As previously mentioned, the designation "citizen-wife" was merely a title conferred on the wife of a male citizen—who was herself the daughter of a male citizen —so that she could bear the much-coveted male citizen.

Thus, unsurprisingly, the all-important area of sacrifice —-vital to the health and prosperity of the *polis*— was the purview of the male citizen. Although women had access to knives for cooking their daily meals, they were wholly excluded from the realm of sacrifice. Detienne remarks: "*Just as women are without political rights, reserved for male citizens, they are also kept apart from altars, meats, and blood.*"[239] To be sure, women were strictly prohibited from using the instruments of death: namely sacrificial sword-like knives (*kopis*) —- even priestesses were forbidden to make sacrifices in some city-states. Since it was entirely incongruous with the ideal feminine qualities of subservience and tranquility, the notion of women brandishing instruments of death was the stuff of nightmares for men. Perhaps especially since Demeter was goddess of the harvest it had long been assumed by scholars that the festival—like all other feminine festivals—dined on vegetarian fare. But such was not the case.

It is now acknowledged that citizen-wives performed sacrifices, and thus required access to these murderous implements. Archaeological evidence discovered at various Demeter sanctuaries throughout the Greek world now demonstrates that full-grown sows were killed in a sacrificial manner, using sacrificial knives.

Furthermore, literary artifacts record meat-eating by the women of the Thesmophoria. Plutarch reports: *"Why at Eretria do the women of the Thesmophoria cook meat in the sun instead of roasting it on the fire?"*[240] That women were eating meat at their festival is indicative

---

239   Detienne, 131.

240   Harrison,130, Detienne, 133.

that they sacrificed animals, and therefore had access to instruments of death and the ability to inflict violence.

In the previous story about Aristomenes, Pausanias confirms this with a passing remark that the citizen-wives had been sacrificing animals, and were thus armed when Aristomenes and his men came upon them. Even the Lucian scholiast—the source for most of what is known about the rites of the Thesmophoria—corroborates that in addition to eating meat, the citizen- wives made sacrifices themselves.[241] Unique among fertility festivals, the Thesmophoria was the *only* feminine cult in the Greek world where sacrifices were performed in secret, without male authority. The confidence that citizen-wives made sacrifices at the Thesmophoria cues prominent classics professor Matthew Dillon to opine: "*There is nothing in the stories that mitigates against believing that women could slay animals except for the notion that women should not do so.*"[242]

According to literary and epigraphic evidence, in most city-states, full-grown sows were sacrificed by the citizen-wives at the Thesmophoria.[243] On the final day of the celebration, the citizen-wives enjoyed roasted

---

241   Stallsmith 3-4.
242   Dillon, *Girls and Women in Classical Greece* 116.
243   However, it should be noted that in the case of the polis of Delos accounting records indicate that the services of a *mageiros* (butcher) was used— presumably to sacrifice the sows.

pig as part of their culminating feast. The mother pigs, however, were not the only swine sacrificed. At some point before the festival, hundreds of piglets were killed when they were thrown into caverns. This type of sacrifice is depicted on an Athenian *lekythos,* showing a disciple crouched over a cavern holding a piglet by his tail before flinging him into the dark and deep recesses of the cavern or *megara (*see Figure 21).[244] Always part of the Thesmophorion shrine where the Thesmophoria was celebrated, the cavern symbolized Demeter's womb. Detienne claims that sacrificing piglets in this manner did not require knives or spits since these animals were simply thrown into the cavern. The piglets, in fact, were killed not for alimentary purposes but because of the sanctity of their rotted remains.[245] Their remains would be retrieved at a later date and become part of the "sacred compost," an offering to the double goddesses in one of the sacred rites.

But not all scholars are in agreement on the type of death the piglets suffered. Dillon suggests that the animals must have been eviscerated before being tossed into the caverns since it would have taken too long for their bodies to decompose otherwise.[246]

244　Some contend that the animal depicted is a dog, not a piglet, and that the woman is an adherent of a festival honoring Hekate–a Titan goddess connected with the underworld.

245　Detienne, 129-130.

246　Dillon, 116.

The reasoning is that there may not have been much time between killing the piglets and scooping up of their remains, thus a high rate of decomposition was essential. It is supposed that even Pausanias believed the animals were eviscerated.[247] Moreover, dozens of small terracotta piglets, with their stomachs slit lengthwise and their organs exposed, have been found at various Demeter sanctuaries throughout the Greek world. These figurines could be indicative of the method in which the piglets met their end. Moreover, Dillon suggests that the clay statues may have been used as a substitution for the real thing.[248] Scattering clay replicas of sacrificial animals in place of the dead animals is something that occasionally occurred in Greek religion. However, because pig remains are part of the "sacred compost" to the double goddesses —hence essential to the health and well-being of the *polis*— some have questioned if the clay substitution would have occurred at the Thesmophoria. Nevertheless, both speculations could be true as this could be another instance where the rites varied from one *polis* to the next or from time to time, depending on the supply of the animals.

Two other common figurines indicative of sacrifice have appeared in Demeter sanctuaries: the first is of a woman carrying a piglet (see Figure 22) and the second

---

247   Ibid, 115.
248   Ibid, 114.

is a figurine of a woman carrying a piglet with one hand and a torch with the other. Presumably, in an effort to increase the fertility of the crops and of themselves, the women in the figurines are carrying the sacrificed piglet as a gift to Demeter.[249]

The Comedy of Sacrifice

The theme of sacrifice comes up in Aristophanes' *Thesmophoriazusae* when the in-law Mnesilochos, who has been impersonating a female disciple at the ritual, is found to be an imposter. In order to keep himself from getting attacked by the armed and dangerous citizen-wives, he snatches a baby from one of the celebrants and threatens to sacrifice it at the altar. "*You'll never feed this baby another sop unless you let me go; nay here atop these thigh bones by this knife stricken, shall its veins run red. Exsanginate the altar.*"[250] Terror of the armed citizen-wife celebrants compels Mnesilochos to stab the hapless infant. To Mnesilochos' great surprise, upon doing so, the "infant " turns out to be nothing more than a wineskin wrapped in swathing. Throughout the play, the citizen-wives are facetiously depicted as enjoying alcohol inappropriately thus Mica—the infant's mother

249   Dillon, 109-119.
250   Aristophanes, "Thesmophoriazusae" lines 755-756.

is deeply distressed about the perforated wineskin.[251] While making every effort to catch the *"precious liquid"* she cries: *"Give me the blood-bowl so at least I can collect my own little one's blood."*[252] In this spoof of piglet sacrifice (see Figure 23), Detienne notes that this act would have no comic effect if the spilled blood were inconsistent with the practices of the Thesmophoria itself.[253]

Since they were secret and known only to citizen wives, Aristophanes cannot provide details of the rites, but it was no mystery that pigs were involved. Thus, stabbing the wineskin can be seen to resemble stabbing a piglet which the citizen-wives would likely have done at the festival. On account of their small size, the female adherents would have had no difficulty carrying out the sacrifice of the piglets. Nevertheless, the infamy was not in killing the animals, as much as in women— an oppressed and largely segregated population— handling instruments of death.

In her seminal book, *Citizen Bacchae*, Goff refers to the *Thesmophoriazusae* as part comedy and part tragedy, opining that the tragic portion represents the grievous narratives of the fate of Battus and Aristomenes which

---

251   Caring more about wine being spilled than her child's blood, Mica's reaction is an example of Aristophanes having fun at the expense of the serious and sacred all-female Thesmophoria.

252   Ibid, 756.

253   Detienne,135.

underpins the satire.[254] Doubtless, Aristophanes struck a nerve in the hearts of Greek men—by exemplifying the ferocity of the women of the Thesmophoria. The audience, overwhelmingly—if not entirely— composed of men, would have been all too familiar with the stories of female savagery inherent in the Thesmophoria. In discussing the threat of the Thesmophoria to patriarchy Zeitlin argues:

> *Inherent in this harnessing of the powers of female fecundity which necessitates an active even violent role for women is the anxiety which surrounds the giving of power to women, power that is as close to parthenogenesis as possible... this threat recalls the continuing Greek fantasy, the Amazon complex....which envisions a city, a society, an alternative structure, composed only of women and innately hostile to men.* [255]

The androcentric powers of ancient Greece were threatened by an imagined race of women on equal footing with them, thus undermining the viability of patrilineal descent in which their power rested. Though they were suspicious of the Thesmophoria's subversive nature, because it was the most prominent of all feminine fertility cults, men could not oppose it.

---

254   Goff, 364.

255   Zeitlin, 1982, 146.

In contrast, citizen-wives who spent the majority of the year in subjugation were empowered by their participation in the prehistoric Thesmophoria—a festival which not only celebrated their powers of reproduction, but evoked a time before the social construct of marriage, a time when women led independent lives. Even though their power was provisional, an oppressed feminine community, free from the shackles of male authority and armed to the teeth, was a genuine threat to the androcentric rule of ancient Greece. The stories of their violence against men— historical or not—- exemplify that the rebellious and clandestine cult was both fear-inducing and a force with which to be reckoned.

CONCLUSION

THE JOURNEY HOME

Culturally, religions more closely reflect the lives of early adherents than the power of their almighty deities. This appears most strongly apparent with the feminine cult festival of the Thesmophoria, in which ancient Greek women found relevance and meaning in a prehistoric agrarian fertility rite. Before being yoked to the patriarchal bond of marriage, the Thesmophoria evoked an era when women had agency in all facets of their lives, enabling the citizen-wife disciples to envision a new reality they might otherwise not possess in the hyper-patriarchal world in which they lived. Confined to the margins of society, ironically, it was the strict division of gender roles denying women agency that gave them an opportunity to exploit the only power they possessed—their sacralized fertility.

The Greeks' non-arable land encouraged a preoccupation with fertility, giving voice to the ordinarily silent half who were its natural agents. Of all the deities, Demeter loomed largest as the chief fertility deity on whose good graces they were most dependent. As one of the oldest of the Olympians, Demeter's origins date back to the Minoan goddess cults. Like much of Greek literature, aspects of Demeter's myth stem from the oral tradition thus are of primeval antiquity. When vanquished kingdoms became absorbed by the invading Mycenaeans, goddess worship was suppressed as invader gods raped or married indigenous goddesses, thereby subordinating them. In fact, the legends of goddess rape signaled the end of matriarchy or matriliny and ushered in patriarchy where kidnapping-cum-marriage would become quotidian. As an expression of cultural memory, prehistoric history melded into mythology, oftentimes making it difficult to differentiate one from the other. This tradition is especially true in the Greek world where lives were principally informed by "myth-history."

Penned in the seventh century BCE, the *Homeric Hymn to Demeter* is one of humankind's oldest literary compositions, evoking early agrarian rituals which may have preceded it by thousands of years. Told from the perspective of the double goddesses, the *Hymn* is a woman's tale addressing such feminine concerns as marriage, agriculture, and sacrifice, whereas the males in the story represent a dark force worthy of repelling.

Demeter's story closely mirrored women's own. Yet, despite Demeter's anguish and suffering at the cruel loss of her daughter, it is only after she exercises her power of fertility—an ability she had possessed all along—-that Demeter is able to negotiate Persephone's release. Is it any wonder that women could identify with Demeter's plight which nearly illustrated their own? Markedly, Demeter does something never seen before in Greek mythology—she resists the will of the patriarch and survives! Not only does Demeter live to tell the tale but she very nearly beats Zeus at his own game. For the majority of the year, Persephone abides with her mother in the light of her mother's earthly domain. Women found resonance in the myth. Facing insurmountable obstacles, like Demeter, they too could use the power of fertility to their advantage.

While women found empowerment in the origins, and meaning in the myth, they found a voice in the prehistoric ritual. Representing an era when women's roles were supreme, even in the ancient world the ritual practice of the Thesmophoria was considered "*of immemorial antiquity.*"[256]Imparted to the early disciples by Demeter herself, they kept their faith throughout the ages with the rites safeguarded from one generation to the next. Although their lives were greatly diminished over the millennia, the citizen-wives were entrusted

256   Harrison, 124.

with the greatest of humankind's mysteries—secrets of how life itself is encouraged —- and found expression by mirroring the worship practices of their powerful primordial foremothers.

Over the course of the festival, in pious acts of mimesis to Demeter, the women mourned and prayed, fasted and indulged, sacrificed and nurtured, laughed and cried, cursed and shared secrets; celebrating their feminine agency throughout. Handling death in order to bring forth life, the disciples helped Demeter fertilize the earth in order to encourage an abundant harvest.

Moreover, the women were united not only with the cycles of nature, which the double goddesses personified, but also with each other by sharing methods to control their fertility through the use of plants. Though the rites of the Thesmophoria were driven by life cycles, the rites of the Eleusinian Mysteries were more concerned with the notion of life after death, illustrating that while there were some similarities between the two festivals, there were more differences. Long considered the male answer to the Thesmophoria, the disparity could be attributed to male dominance which would eventually become intrinsic within the Mysteries.

Despite its provisional authority, the Thesmophoria made its presence felt by turning the power dynamics between the sexes on its head. Although men supported the Thesmophoria because its celebration was necessary for the health and well-being of the polis, they did so with wary suspicion, which is confirmed by the stories about the savagery of citizen-wives toward male interlopers. The adherents of the Thesmophoria formed a united feminine community in which its members were in charge of running the festival as an *ad hoc* gynocracy. They held elections, drafted proposals, kept accounting, made sacrifices, and practiced sacred feminine ritual, all without male interference. In a tight-knit feminine community that met yearly, the women became confidants. Could experienced members have taught novices ways to utilize plants to aid their reproductive agency? Might old friends have come together to share child-birthing techniques? In an example of art imitating life, were long-lost daughters reunited with their beloved mothers in a bond more enduring than marriage? Certainly, stories of deep and cultural significance had been shared for Demeter and Persephone's struggles were their own.

Ultimately their work was done. The morning after the final night's concluding ceremony, the citizen-wives began to pack for home. After all, they had *oikos* to return to; homes where husbands and children were dependent on them. Filing out processionally, the disciples descended Demeter's sanctuary, many carrying their primordial makeshift huts that served as their homes during the festival. As they made their way into town, were they joyfully singing the *Hymn* in praise of Demeter, or were they solemnly chanting?

We can only guess. The citizen-wives must have felt a deep sense of accomplishment on a job well done. On account of their hard work, the festival was a success: a favorable portent ensuring the strength of the seeds in the forthcoming sowing season, which would, in turn, ensure their own reproductive strength. From near and from far, spectators enthusiastically lined the streets in order to watch the pious women make their descent. Everyone knew the critical part the women played and were grateful for their contribution. As adherents of the Thesmophoria, their roles were gargantuan. In their hands was nothing less than the future health and prosperity of the *polis*, so all-important was crop and human fertility in ancient Greece.

SOURCES AND FURTHER READING

Aeschylus. *The Suppliant Maidens*. Translated by David Greene and Richard Lattimore. Chicago & London: The University of Chicago Press, 2013.

Aristophanes. *Ecclesiazusae.* http://classics.mit.edu/ Aristophanes/eccles.html

_____ *Thesmophoriazusae*. Edited by Alan H. Sommerstein. Warminster, England: Aris & Phillips Ltd, 1994.

Aristotle. *Politics.* Translated by H. Rackham. Cambridge, MA: Harvard University Press, 1944.

Bernal, Martin. *Black Athena: The Afroasiatic Roots of Classical Civilization*. London: Vintage Books, 1987.

Blundell, Sue. *The Origins of Civilization in Greek and Roman Thought.* (London: Routledge, 1989), 534-535.

_____ *Women in Ancient Greece*. Cambridge: Harvard University Press, 1995

Bonner, Campbell. "The Danaid Myth." *Transactions and Proceedings of the American Philological Association,* 31 (1900), 28-36.

Bowden, Hugh. *Mystery Cults of the Ancient World*. London: Thames & Hudson Ltd, 2010.

Burkert, Walter. *Greek Religion*. Cambridge: Harvard University Press, 1985.

Cantarella, Eva. "Dangling Virgins: Myths, RItual and the Place of Women in Ancient Greece." *Poetics Today* 6 no ½ (1985): 91-101.

Carus, Paul. "The Greek Mysteries, A Preparation for Christianity." *The Monist* 11, no. 1 (October,1900): 87. https://www.jstor.org/stable/27899193.

Clinton, Kevin. "Epiphany in the Eleusinian Mysteries." *Illinois Classical Studies* 29 (2004): 85–109. http://www.jstor.org/stable/23065342.

_____ *Myth and Cult: The Iconography of the Eleusinian Mysteries*. Stockholm: Svenska Institute I Athen, 1990.

_____ "The Sanctuary of Demeter and Kore at Eleusis," In *Greek Sanctuaries: New Approaches*,

Edited by Nanno Marinatos and Robin Hagg. (London: Routledge, 1993), 110-124.

Connelly, Joan Breton. *Portrait of a Priestess: Women and Ritual in Ancient Greece.* Princeton: Princeton University Press, 2007.

Cook, Arthur Bernard. *Zeus: A Study in Ancient Religion*. Cambridge: Cambridge University Press, 1940. Quoted in Marguerite Rigoglioso, Virgin Mother Goddesses of Antiquity. New York: Palgrave MacMillan, 2010.

Daly, Kathleen. *Greek and Roman Mythology A-Z.* Revised by Marian Rangel. New York: Chelsea House Publication, 2009.

Demosthenes. *Speeches Against Neaera*. Austin, TX: University of Texas Press: 2003.

Detienne, Marcel. "The Violence of Wellborn Ladies: Women in the Thesmophoria." In *The Cuisine of Sacrificing Among the Greeks*, edited by Marcel Detienne and Jean-Pierre Vernant, trans by Paula Wissing, 129-147. Chicago: University of Chicago Press, 1989.

Dillon, Matthew. *Girls and Women in Classical Greek Religion*. London: Routledge, 2002.

Diodorus Siculus. *Bibliotheca Historia*. 5.4-7. Quoted in Burkert, *Greek Religion*. Cambridge: Harvard University Press, 1985.

Dobson, Marcia W. D-S. "Ritual Death, Patriarchal Violence, and Female Relationships In the Hymn to Demeter and Ianna." *NWSA Journal*, 4 no. 1 (Spring 1992): 42-58. http://www.jstor.org/stable/4316175.

Euripides. *Ion.* Translated. by Ronald Frederick Willetts. Chicago: Chicago University Press, 1958.

_____ *Medea.* Translated and Edited by Sheila Murnaghan. New York: W. W. Norton & Company, 2018.

_____ *The Trojan Women*. Edited by David Greene and Richard Lattimore. Chicago: Chicago University Press, 1958.

Evans, Nancy. "Sanctuaries, Sacrifices, and the Eleusinian Mysteries." *Numen* 49, no. 3 (2002): 227-254. http://www.jstor.com/stable/3270542.

Filonik, Jakub. "Athenian Impiety Trials: A Reappraisal." *ResearchGate*

Foley, Helene P. *The Homeric Hymn to Demeter: Translation, Commentary, and Interpretive*

Essays. Princeton, NJ: Princeton University Press, 1994.

Fortunato, Laura. "Reconstructing the History of Marriage Strategies in Indo-European Speaking Societies: Monogamy and Polygamy." *Human Biology.* 1 no. 83 (Feb, 2011). http://www.ncbi.nih.gov/pubmed/21453006.

Frazer, James. *The Golden Bough.* London: Summit Classic Press, 2012.

Gagne, Renaud. "Mystery Inquisitors: Performance, Authority and Sacrilege at Eleusis," *Classical Antiquity,* 28, no.2 (October 2009), 211-247.

Gimbutas, Marija. *The Goddesses and Gods of Old Europe: Myth and Cult Images 6500-3500 BCE.* Berkeley: University of California Press, 1982.

_____ *The Living Goddess.* Edited by Miriam Robbins Dexter. Berkeley: University of California Press, 2001.

Goff, Barbara. *Citizen Bacchae: Women's Ritual Practice in Ancient Greece.* Berkeley: University of California Press, 2004.

Graeber, David, and David Wengrow. *The Dawn of Everything: A New History of Humanity.* New York: Farrar, Straus, and Giroux, 2021.

Graf, Fritz "Eleusis und die orphische Dichtung Athens im vorbellenistischer Zeit." Quoted in Lowe, N. J. "Thesmophoria and Haloa: Myth, Physics and Mysteries," in *The Sacred and the Feminine in Ancient Greece,* edited by Sue Blundell and Margaret Williamson, 149-173. London: Rutledge, 1998.

_____ *Greek Mythology–An Introduction.* Trans. Thomas Marier. Munich: The Johns Hopkins University Press, 1993.

Graves, Robert. "Introduction." In the *New Larousse Encyclopedia of Mythology*, translated By Richard Aldington and Delano Ames, v. London: Hamlyn, 1968.

Griffin, R. Drew. "Cannibal Demeter and the Thesmophoria Pigs," T*he Classical Journal* 111, n. 1 (December 2015), 137. https://www.jstor.org/stable/10.5184/classicalj.111.2.0129

Hanson, Victor Davis. *A War Like No Other: How the Athenians and Spartans Fought The Peloponnesian War*. New York: Random House, 2005.

_____ *The Other Greeks: The Family Farm and the Agrarian Roots of Western Civilization*. Berkeley: University of California Press, 1999.

Harrison, Jane Ellen. *Prolegomena to the Study of Greek Religion*. New York: Forgotten Books, 1903.

Herodotus. *The Histories.* In Jon D. Mikalson, *Herodotus and Religion in the Persian Wars.* (Chapell Hill: The University of North Carolina Press, 2003).

Hesiod. *Theogony.* Translated by Dorothea Wender. London: Penguin Books, 1982.

Homer. *The Odyssey*. Translated by Robert Fagles. New York: Penguin Books, 1996.

_____ *The Odyssey*. Translated by Emily Wilson. New York: W.W. Norton & Co., 2018.

Jung, Carl. "Essays on a Science of Mythology." Quoted in Carl Kerenyi, *Eleusis: Archetypal Image of Mother and Daughter*. Princeton: Princeton University Press, 1967.

Keller, Mara Lynn. "The Eleusinian Mysteries of Demeter and Persephone: Fertility, Sexuality and Rebirth." *Journal of Feminist Studies* in Religion 4, no. 1 (Spring, 1988). http://www.jstor.org/stable/25002068.

Kerenyi, Carl. *Eleusis: Archetypal Image of Mother and Daughter*. Princeton: Princeton University Press, 1967.

_____ *Zeus and Hera: Archetypal Image of Father, Husband, and Wife.* Princeton: Princeton University Press, 1975.

Kirk, G. S. *Myth: Its Meanings & Functions in Ancient Greece & Other Cultures.* London Cambridge University Press, 1970.

Lowe, N.J. "Thesmophoria and Haloa: Myth, Physics, and Mysteries," In *The Sacred and The feminine in Ancient Greece,* edited by Sue Blundell and Margeret Williamson, 149-173. London: Routledge, 1998.

Lucian, Scholiast to Dialogue Meretricii 2.1. Quoted in Jane Ellen Harrison, *Prolegomena to the Study of Greek Religion.* New York: Forgotten Books, 1903.

Mark, Joshua J. "The Eleusinian Mysteries RItes of Demeter." https://www.worldhistory.org/article/32/the-eleusinian-mysteries-the-rites-of-demeter/

McClure, Laura. *Spoken Like a Woman: Speech and Gender in Athenian Drama.* Princeton: Princeton University Press, 1999.

Meador, De Shong Betty. *Uncursing the Dark.* Wilmette, Illinois: Chiron Publications, 1994.

Meyer, Marvin W. T*he Ancient Mysteries Sourcebook: Sacred Texts of the Mystery Religions of the Ancient Mediterranean World.* San Francisco: Harper & Row Publishers, 1997.

Nagy, Gregory. *The Homeric Hymn to Demeter.* https://chs.harvard.edu/primary-source/homeric-hymn-to-demeter-sb/

Neumann, Erich. *Amore and Psyche: The Psychic Development of the Feminine.* New York: Princeton University Press, 1956.

Nicolson, Adam. *The Mighty Dead: Why Homer Matters.* London: Williams Collins, 2015.

Nixon, Lucia. "The Cults of Demeter and Kore." In *Women in Antiquity: New Assessments*, edited by Richard Hawley and Barbara Levick. 76-93. London: Routledge, 1995.

Osborne, Robin. "Women and Sacrifice in Classical Greece." *The Classical Quarterly* 43, no. 2 (1993), 392-405. http://www.jstor.org/stable/639178.

Otto, Walter F. "The Meaning of the Eleusinian Mysteries." In *The Mysteries: Paper From the Eranos Yearbook*, edited by Joseph Campbell, 14-31. New York: Princeton University Press, 1955.

Parke, H. W. *Festivals of the Athenians*. London: Thames and Hudson, Ltd., 1977.

Plutarch. *Moralia*. Loeb Classical Library: 1936.

Pomeroy, Sarah B. *Goddesses, Whores, Wives, and Slaves: Women in Antiquity.* New York: Schocken Books, 1975.

_____ *Women In Hellenistic Egypt.* New York: Schocken Books, 1984.

Pratt, Louise. "The Old Women of Ancient Greece and the Homeric Hymn to Demeter. *Transactions of the American Philological Association* 130, no. 2 (2000). http://www.jstor.org/stable/284305.

Rigoglioso, Marguerite. *Virgin Mother Goddesses of Antiquity*. New York: PalgraveMacMillan, 2010.

_____ "Persephone's Sacred Lake." *Journal of Feminist Studies* 21, no.2 (Fall 2005) http://www.jstor.org/stable/25002531

Schaps, David. "The Women of Greece in Wartime." *Classical Philology* 77, no. 3 (1982). http://www.jstor.org/stable/270245.

Schmidt, Wilhelm. *The Origin of the Idea of God*. Quoted in Joseph Campbell, *Primitive Mythology*. New York: Penguin Group, 1969.

Seutonius. *Lives of the Twelve Caesars.* Translated by H.M. Bird. London: Wordsworth Editions Limited, 1997.

Simon, Erika. *Festivals of Attica: An Archaeological Commentary,* Madison, Wisconsin: University of Wisconsin Press, 1983.

Sourvinou-Inwood, Christiane. "Aspects of the Eleusinian Cult." In G*reek Mysteries: The Archaeology and Ritual of Ancient Greek Secret Cults*, edited by Michael B. Cosmopoulos, 25-47. London: Routledge, 2003.

Stallsmith, Allaire B. "Interpreting the Athenian Thesmophoria." *Classical Bulletin* 84.1 (2009). https://www.academia.edu/2381368/ Interpreting_the_Athenian_Thesmophoria

Stehle, Eva. "Thesmophoria and Eleusinian Mysteries: The Fascination of Women's Secret Ritual." In *Finding Persephone: Women's Ritual in the Ancient Mediterranean,* edited by Maryline Parca and Angeliki Tzanetou, 165-185. Bloomington, Indiana: Indiana University Press, 2007.

Stone, Merlin. *When God Was a Woman.* Orlando, Florida: Harcourt, Inc., 1976.

Thomson, George. *Aeschylus and Athens: The Classic Study in the Social Origins Of Drama.* New York: The Universal Library, 1968.

Thompson, Homer A. "Pynx and Thesmophorian." *Hesperia: The American School of Classical Studies at Athens*, 5, no. 2., (1936), 151-200.

Tully, Carolyn. "Demeter's Wrath: How the Eleusinian Mysteries Attempted to Cheat Death", In *Memento Mori* Edited by. Kim Huggens. London: Avalonia, 2012. 144-152

Tzanetou, Angeliki. "Something to do with Demeter: Ritual and Performance in Aristophanes' *Women of the Thesmophoria*." *The American Journal of Philology* 123, no.3 (Autumn 2002). http://www.jstor.org/stable/1561692.

Versnel, H. S. "The Festival of Bona Dea and the Thesmophoria." *Greece & Rome,* 39 (April 1992).

Winkler, John J. *The Constraints of Desire.* New York: Routledge, 1990.

Xenophon, *Oeconomicus* 5.17. Quoted in Victor Hanson, *The Other Greeks: The Family Farm and the Agrarian Roots of Western Civilization.* New York: Simon & Schuster Inc., 1995.

Zeitlin Froma I. "Cultic Models of the Female: Rites of Dionysus and Demeter." *Arethusa* 15, no. 1/2 (1982): 129–57. http://www.jstor.org/stable/26308107.

_____ *Playing the Other*. Chicago: University of Chicago Press, 1996.

www.ingramcontent.com/pod-product-compliance
Lightning Source LLC
Chambersburg PA
CBHW040850120626
46547CB00006B/557